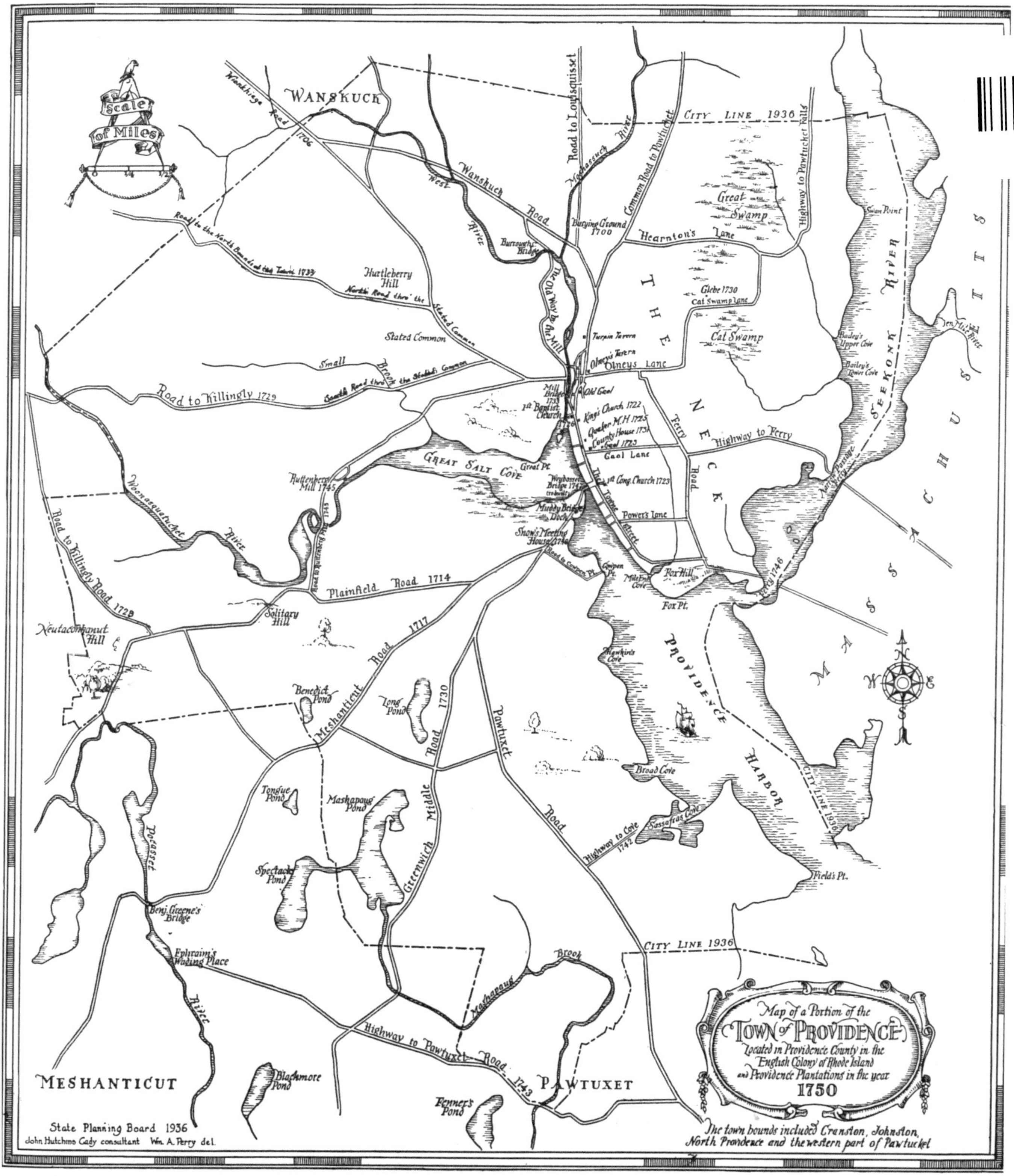
Map of a Portion of the
TOWN of PROVIDENCE
Located in Providence County in the English Colony of Rhode Island and Providence Plantations in the year
1750
The town bounds included Cranston, Johnston, North Providence and the western part of Pawtucket
State Planning Board 1936
John Hutchins Cady consultant Wm. A. Perry del.
Scale of Miles
WANSKUCK
MESHANTICUT
PAWTUXET
THE NECK
PROVIDENCE HARBOR
SEEKONK RIVER
MASSACHUSETTS
CITY LINE 1936
Road to Louisquisset
Common Road to Pawtucket
Highway to Pawtucket Falls
Wanskuck Road
West River
Moshassuck River
Great Swamp
Hearnton's Lane
Burying Ground 1700
Burrough's Bridge
Hurtleberry Hill
Stated Common
Small Brook
Road to Killingly 1729
Glebe 1730
Cat Swamp Lane
Cat Swamp
Turpin Tavern
Olney's Tavern
Olneys Lane
Old Gaol
Mill Bridge
1st. Baptist Church
King's Church 1722
Quaker M.H. 1725
County House 1731
Gaol Lane
Highway to Ferry
Ferry Road
Swan Point
Bailey's Upper Cove
Bailey's Lower Cove
GREAT SALT COVE
Great Pt.
Weybosset Bridge
Muddy Bridge
1st Cong. Church 1723
Powers Lane
Snow's Meeting House
Fox Hill
Fox Pt.
Ruttenberg Mill 1745
Woonasquatucket River
Road to Killingly Road 1729
Plainfield Road 1714
Solitary Hill
Neutaconkanut Hill
Meshanticut Road 1717
Benedict Pond
Long Pond
Middle Road 1730
Pawtuxet Road
Broad Cove
Sassafras Cove
Highway to Cove 1742
Field's Pt.
Tongue Pond
Mashapaug Pond
Spectacle Pond
Greenwich Road
Pocasset River
Benj. Greene's Bridge
Ephraim's Wading Place
Mashapaug Brook
Highway to Pawtuxet Road 1743
Blackmore Pond
Fenner's Pond
CITY LINE 1936

Through Our Eyes: An Indigenous View of Mashapaug Pond

Visit our website at **www.StillwaterPress.com** for more information.

First Stillwater River Publications Edition.
Previously published in 2012 by The Tomaquag Museum and Holly Ewald, Exeter, Rhode Island.

ISBN: 978-1-968548-10-0

Library of Congress Control Number: 2025919994

1 2 3 4 5 6 7 8 9 10
Edited by Dawn Dove, Holly Ewald, and Lorén Spears.
Book design by Leticia Tejada and Matthew St. Jean.
Cover design by Matthew St. Jean.
Published by Stillwater River Publications, West Warwick, RI, USA.

Special thanks to Lu Heintz and the 2025 Providence Commemoration Lab, funded in part by the Mellon Foundation.

Publisher's Cataloging-in-Publication
(Provided by Cassidy Cataloguing Services, Inc.)
Names: Dove, Dawn, editor. | Ewald, Holly, editor. | Spears, Lorén M., 1966- editor.
Title: Through our eyes : an Indigenous view of Mashapaug Pond / edited by Dawn Dove, Holly Ewald, and Lorén Spears.
Description: First Stillwater River Publications edition. | West Warwick, RI, USA : Stillwater River Publications, [2025] | "Previously published in 2012 by The Tomaquag Museum"—Title page verso.
Identifiers: LCCN: 2025919994 | ISBN: 9781968548100 (paperback)
Subjects: LCSH: Narragansett Indians—Rhode Island—Providence County—History. | Indigenous peoples—Rhode Island—Providence County—History. | Indigenous peoples--Rhode Island—Providence County—Poetry. | Indigenous peoples—Rhode Island—Providence County—Pictorial works. | Gorham Manufacturing Company. | Mashapaug Pond (Providence County, R.I.)—Poetry. | Mashapaug Pond (Providence County, R.I.)—Pictorial works. | LCGFT: Poetry. | Illustrated works.
Classification: LCC: E99.N16 T47 2026 | DDC: 974.52--dc23

THROUGH OUR EYES

An Indigenous View *of* Mashapaug Pond

Edited by Dawn Dove, Holly Ewald, and Lorén Spears

TABLE OF CONTENTS

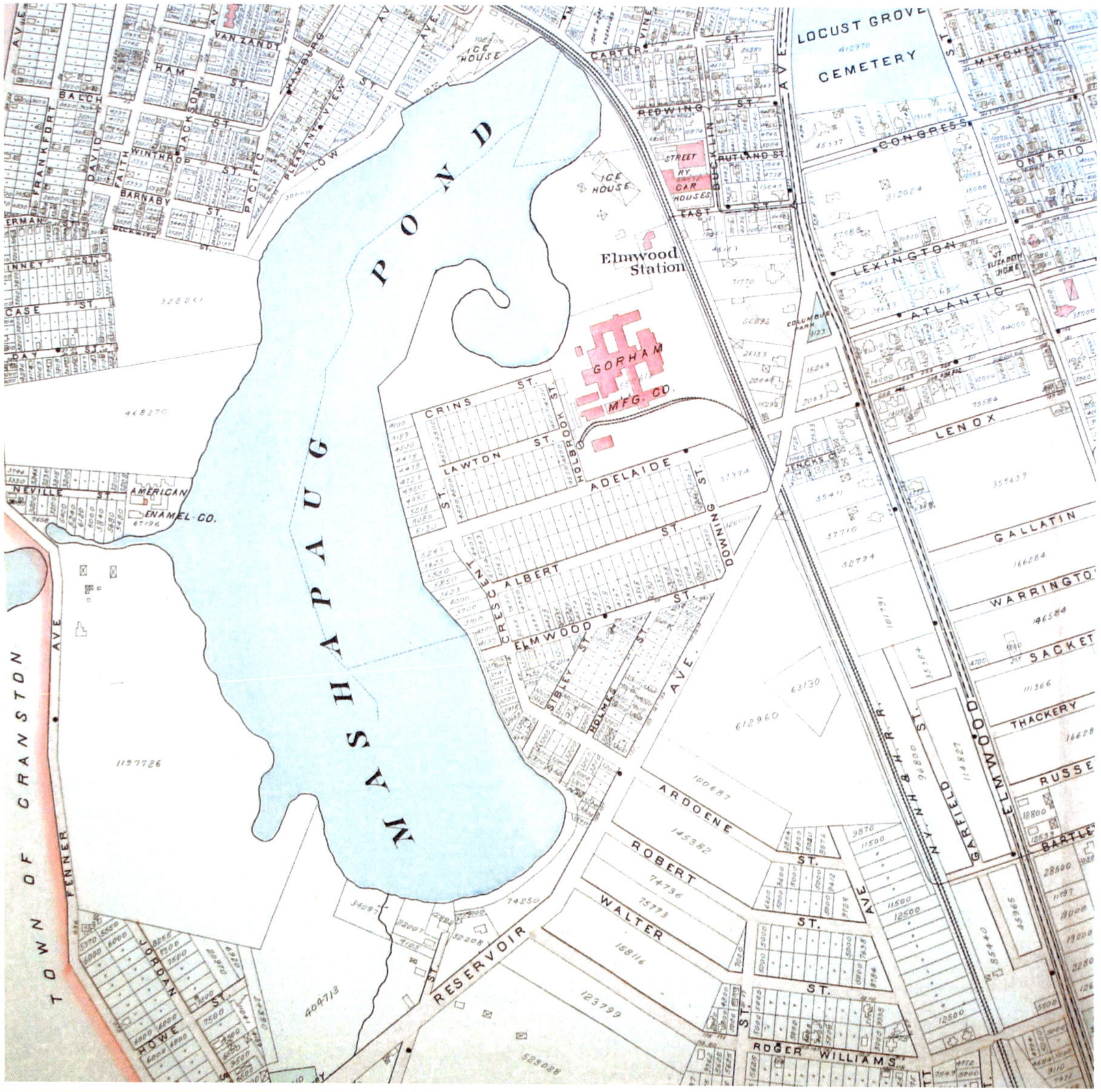
MASHAPAUG POND
LOCUST GROVE CEMETERY
GORHAM MFG. CO.
Elmwood Station
ICE HOUSE
STREET RY CAR HOUSES
AMERICAN ENAMEL CO.
TOWN OF CRANSTON
FENNER AVE
RESERVOIR AVE
ELMWOOD AVE
ROGER WILLIAMS AVE
N.Y. N.H. & H. R.R.
VAN ZANDT
HAM ST.
BALCH
WINTHROP ST.
BARNABY ST.
PACIFIC
PLEASANT VIEW
LOW
CASE ST.
NEVILLE ST.
CARTER
REDWING ST.
RUTLAND ST.
EAST
CONGRESS
MITCHELL
ONTARIO
LEXINGTON
ATLANTIC
LENOX
GALLATIN
WARRINGTON
SACKETT
THACKERY
RUSSELL
BARTLETT
CRINS ST.
LAWTON ST.
HOLBROOK ST.
ADELAIDE
ALBERT ST.
ELMWOOD
CRESCENT
DOWNING ST.
SIBLEY ST.
HOLMES
JENCKS CT.
ARDOENE
ROBERT ST.
WALTER ST.
GARFIELD
JORDAN
HOWE

INTRODUCTION

Mashapaug Pond is the largest body of fresh water in Providence and was a significant site to Indigenous people for centuries before and after the Europeans settled in what is now known as Rhode Island, in 1636. At the turn of the 20th century, Gorham Silver Manufacturing Company built its 37-acre plant on its shores in 1890 and played a vital role in the development of Providence and American Decorative Arts until 1967. Today the waters and soil of Mashapaug Pond suffer from Gorham's silver, copper, and bronze manufacturing processes, as well as from urban storm runoff. This book is intended to immerse readers in Narragansett culture and help them imagine this urban neighborhood pond in the past and the future as a healthy, life-sustaining body of water.

Through Our Eyes is a collection of collages and writing by Indigenous People that envisions what Mashapaug Pond might have been like with their ancestors living on its shores, along with commentary about the pond today. The creative work is supplemented by two factual essays. One is written text by Holly Ewald based on an interview with Narragansett/Niantic elder Paulla Dove Jennings about her vision of Mashapaug Pond as an Indigenous settlement before 1600 and the Narragansett cultures that are present today. Although not an exact quotation text, it is largely based on Paulla Dove Jennings' words. Text has been reorganized to address specific topics. Paulla Dove Jennings approved this version of her stories. The final text is a transcribed presentation by anthropologist Dr. William Simmons about the continued presence of Indigenous People by Mashapaug through the 21st century. It is based on research and oral histories done in the 1980s.

The book project was designed and facilitated by artist Holly Ewald in collaboration with Lorén Spears, Executive Director of the Tomaquag Museum. The collages and writing were created and written by Narragansett people, from ages 8 to 92, who met weekly at the Tomaquag Museum during the fall and winter months of 2010-11. The group visited Mashapaug Pond to acquaint themselves with the ancestral site as well as to photograph and learn about the poor environmental condition of the pond today. Photographing at Arcadia Pond, a much healthier pond near the museum, yielded collage materials as well. Because we wanted the collages and writing presented as a collective vision, attributions for the artwork and writing appear by page number at the end of the book (page 41).

This book is part of an ongoing project led by artist Holly Ewald and the Urban Pond Procession (UPP) to raise awareness about the historical significance and environmental vulnerability of Mashapaug as well as other ponds in the Lower Pawtuxet Watershed. The Urban Pond Procession (UPP) is made up of a revolving group of volunteer artists, scientists, educators, and concerned citizens who are all interested in collaborating to promote the health of these urban ponds. It facilitates workshops for all ages in which participants learn about the ponds' environmental and health issues while making creative props for an annual celebratory procession to raise further awareness and advocate for the ponds' cleanup, both building community and improving the environment. Through these efforts UPP hopes to build stewardship for the ponds' futures.

We thank the following people for their committed participation in this project: Eleanor Dove, Nkéke Waupianoohom Harris, Sherenté Mishitashin Harris, Wesly Jennings, Paulla Dove Jennings, Lynsea Montanari, Laurel Spears, Lorén Spears, Ridge Spears, Robin Spears. We also acknowledge the following people for their support and contribution in bringing this book to final completion: Michael Bell, Rick Benjamin, David Graff, Margaret Klawunn, John McNiff, Lucia O'Reilly, Leticia Tejada, Anne Valk. Thank you to Lu Heinz and Stillwater River Publications for help with the 2025 edition of this book.

Holly Ewald, *Founder, Urban Pond Procession*

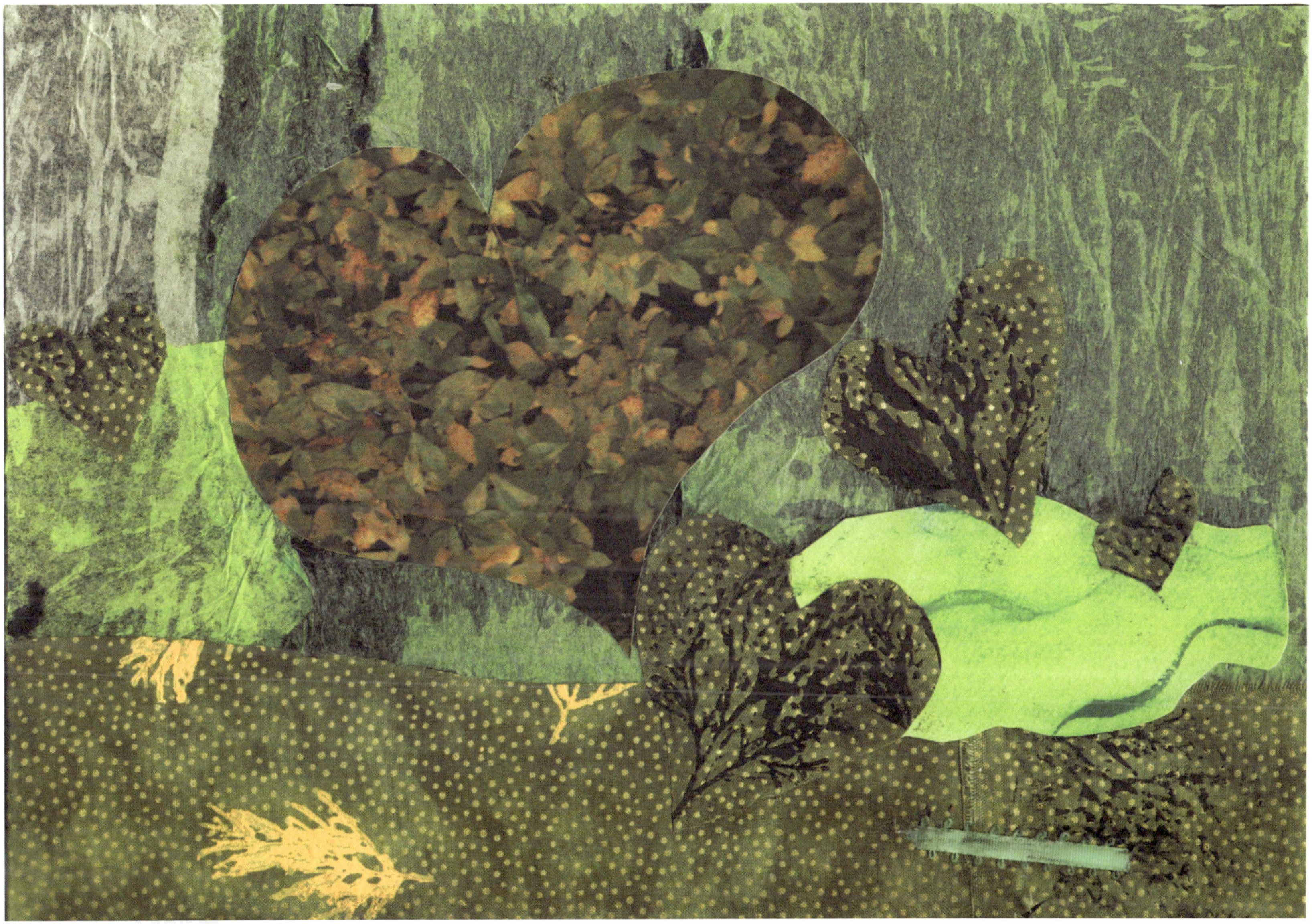

Mashapaug Pond Through Our Eyes: Collages and Writing

Arts and Wellness Participants at Tomaquag Museum

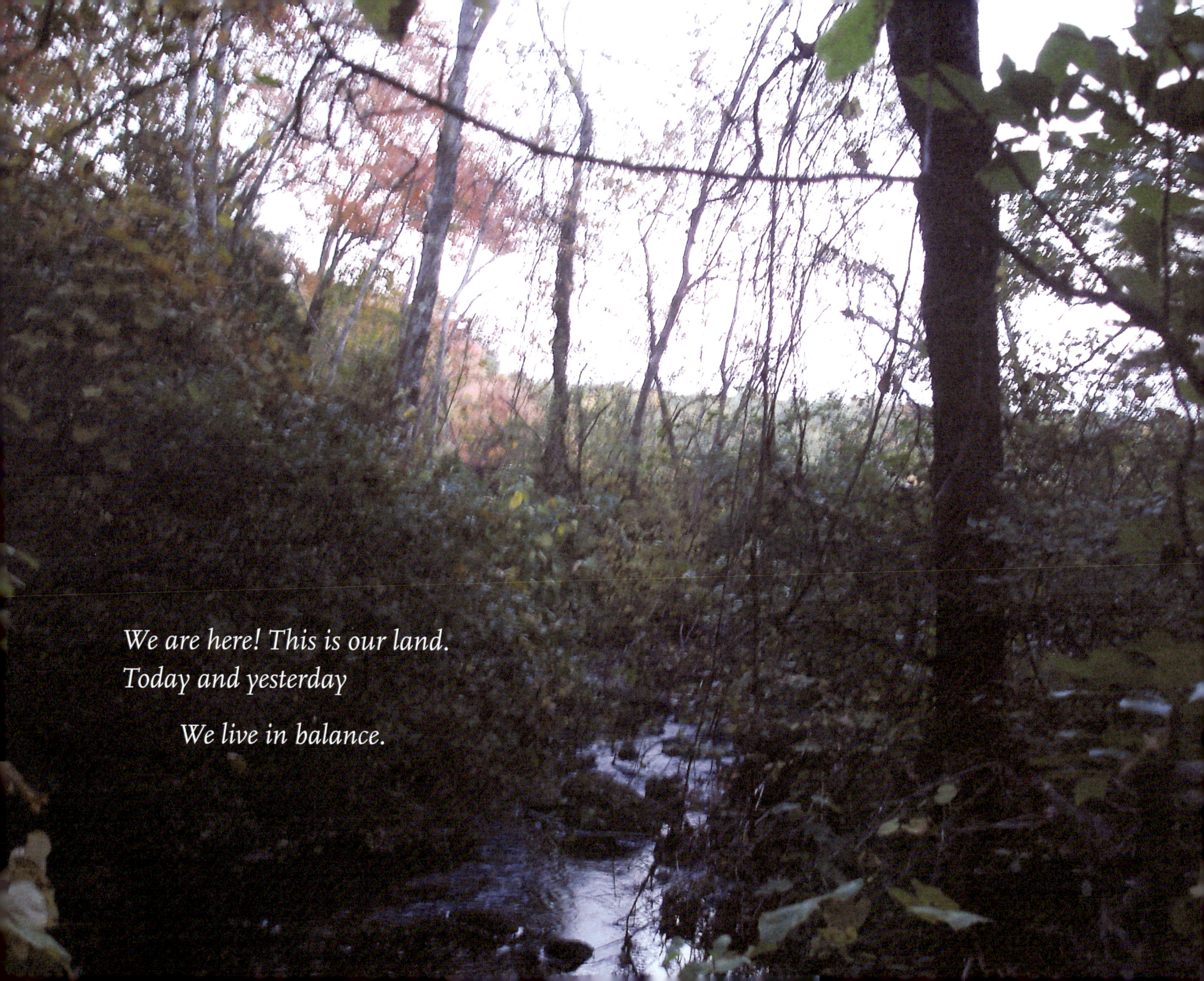

We are here! This is our land.
Today and yesterday

We live in balance.

CIRCLE

Let's walk around the pond.
What do we see?
I see ahtukquag,
        nunaum bulrushes
        nunaum cattail
        nunaum wetu
The ancestors speak to us
Tyaqa Kutussem?

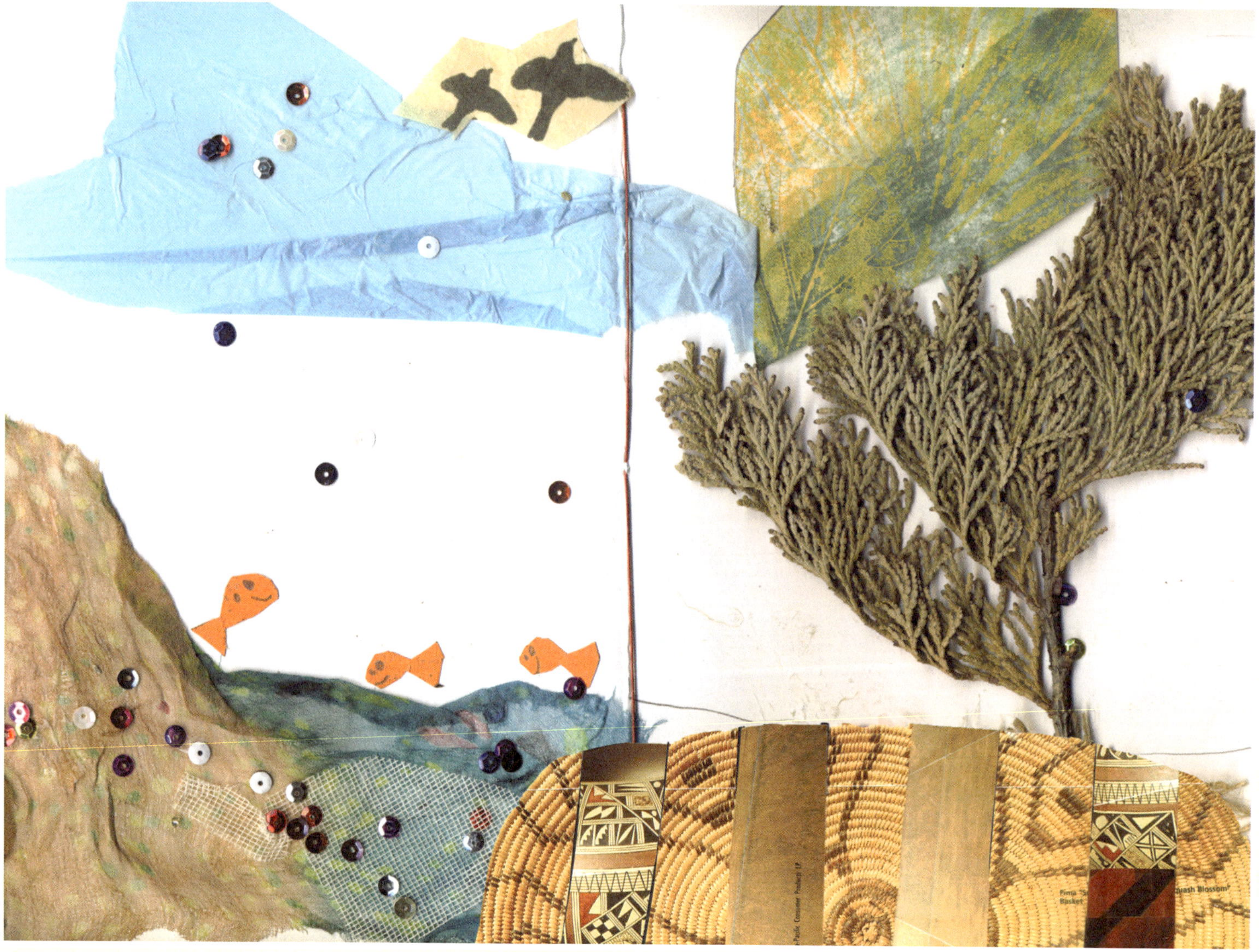

Mashapaug Pond, place of beauty
Summer home—reeds gathered
Winter home—wild turkeys—family together in the longhouse
Spring —fishing and everything coming to life

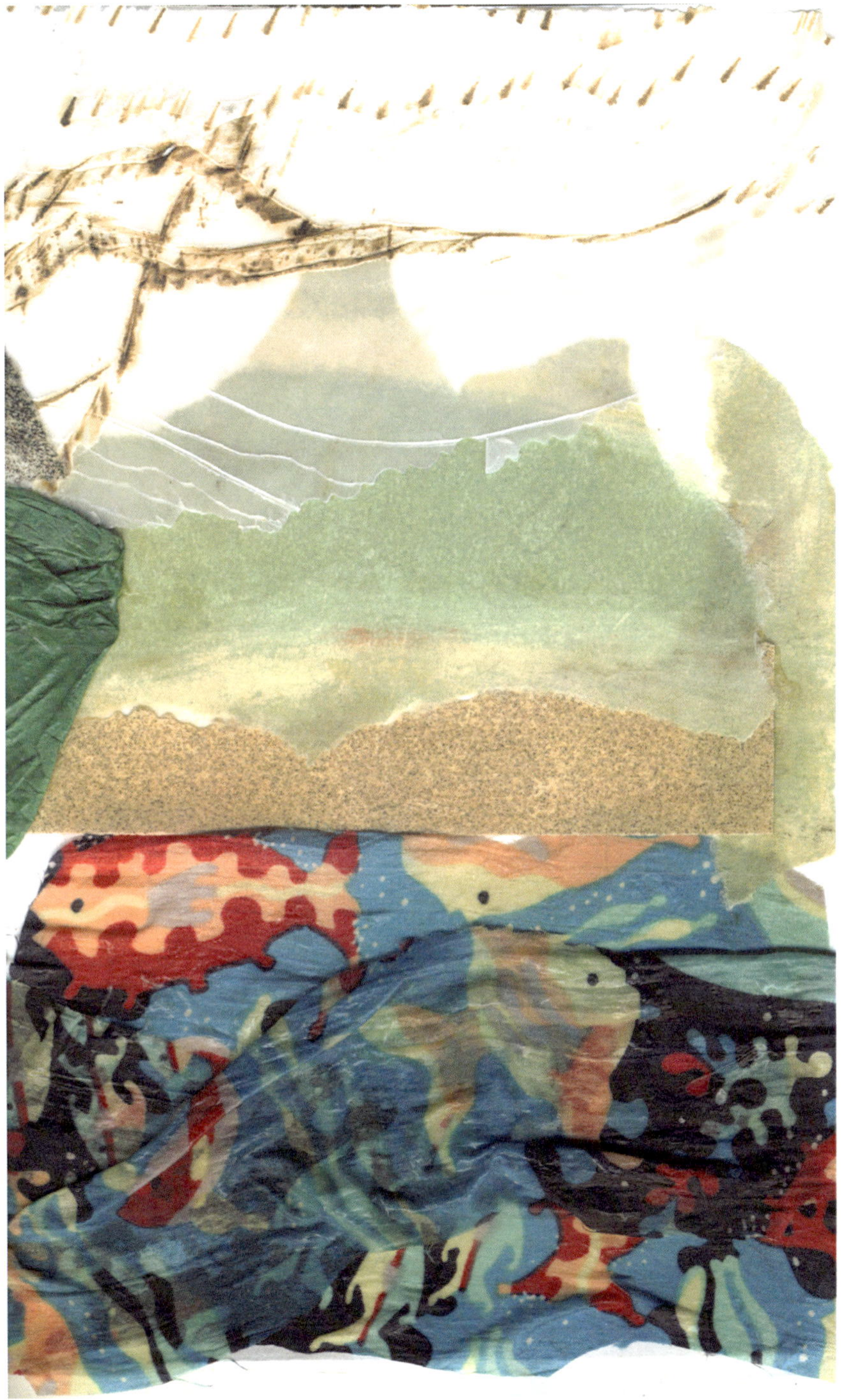

At Mashapaug the family enjoys the day—keesuk
Fishing, gathering, exploring
together they provide for their family and community.
Mashapaug provides what they need.

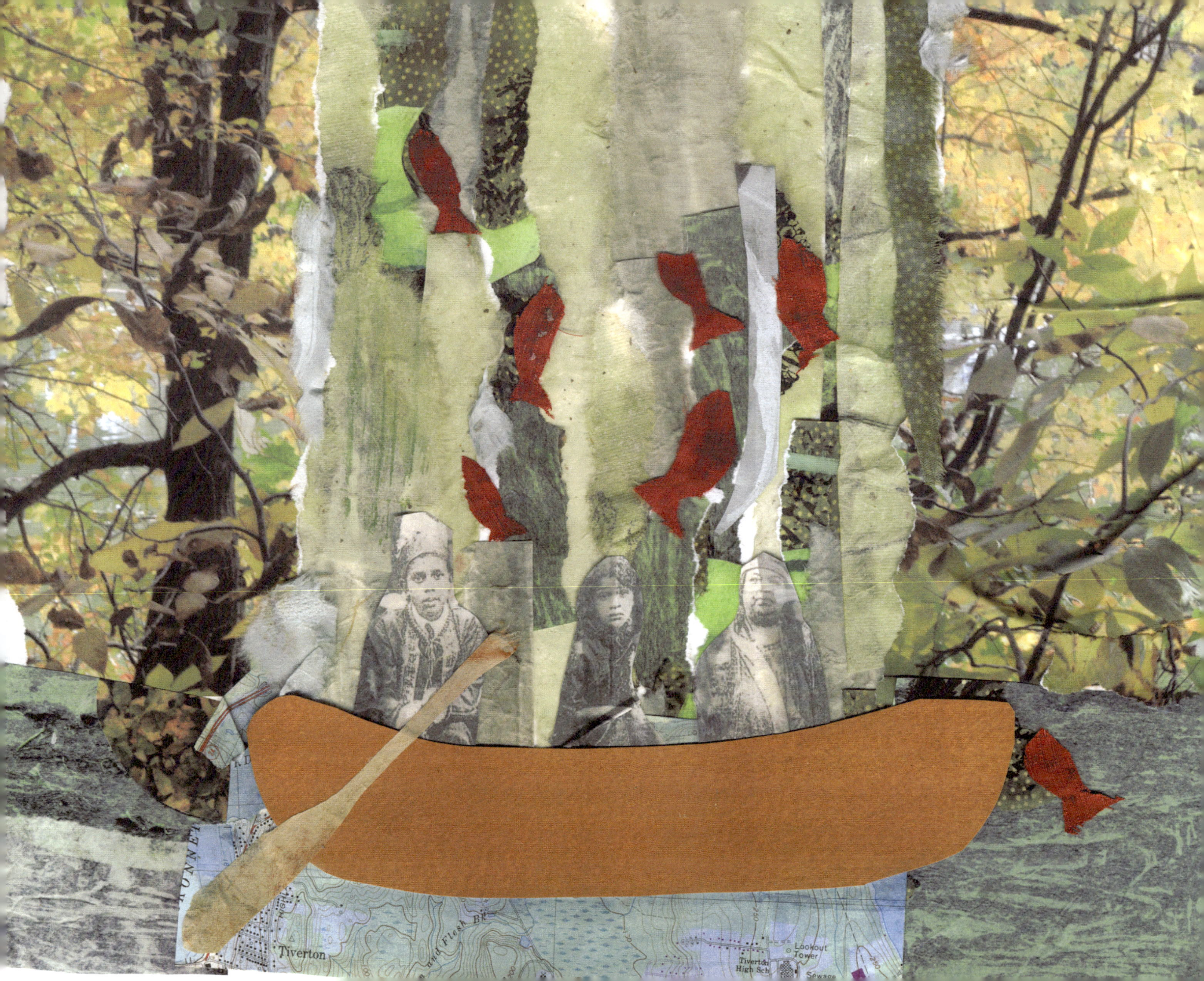
Tiverton
Lookout Tower
Tiverton High Sch

The Spirit of the People
our Ancestors travels with us.
Misquam Red Fish, Red Tears
fall from my heart
We travel together
We travel to meet the spirit people.

Fish so beautiful a creature. Life of many animals depend on them with so much power they journey against the river jumping and swimming to fulfill their drive. A drive so powerful as to disregard their own life so their children can live. They play their part and we play ours. We, like many animals, depend on the salmon for food to live. They taste great. Many will say it tastes great even as the last salmon dies.

Salmon traveling
the salmon people are our
sisters—they are
coming home
See them jump
The canoe is traveling
bringing home the people

I see a canoe in the water this side of the waterfalls. The fish are trying to swim up the falls. The people in the canoe are looking out at the pond to see if there are any fish to be had. I think the fish have outsmarted the people this time by going under the canoe to climb the falls.

Hollow the mushoon
Hollow a cocoon
You're hungry for some food
What to satisfy the mood
Salty waters fill your head
Searching for the fish that's
Red
Leaves crisply crunch beneath your feet
You push your canoe into the neep
You nap inside and start to
Paddle, You're done, you wait
hum and rattle
You hear a splash you turn around,
There is nothing to be found
You turn your head back with much sorrow
Others' food you have to borrow
You don't believe your eyes
splashing salmon to your supper.

I slip on my moccasunash and run towards our mushoon. Neeshwa waves goodbye as Noosh, Pum and I set off. We paddle out to a waterfall. It is hot. As we row under the neepsnon I cleanse myself. The cool sprinkle of water cools me and trickles down my back. We journey forward. Pummukau is almost lulled to sleep by the sway of the boat. When he falls out of the boat Noosh and I pull him up as he laughs. His beautiful laugh fills me with joy. I look forward. I hear dragonflies hum softly over the lily pads. Even though Pum is young and isn't able to speak much he understands and says "I love you!"

We feel a cool breeze and hear tanoquaquas. It is calming and peaceful. We see salmon in the distance. Noosh directs us in that direction. The mishquam are splashing in all directions. Pum gets splashed with water. We pull out our nets and fish. Noosh shows us the tricks and ways to fish and to be sure not to catch too many and to save some for others who come fishing on Mother Earth. Noosh teaches Pum how to spear or net. Pummukau catches 3 little fish. I catch 8 and Noosh catches 14. We return to the shore. Neeshwa sings the stomp dance as we return home.

Nokomis shows us the importance of sharing with all our relations. We share our fish with the poor people of our community. Before we eat Nokomis says a prayer.

Numanutoomun
Nupeeyaumun een keen keesuqat
Nashmee nucheeqanaeetahunaunash
Kuttuppatutumash
Kittantauwat wutchee wamee
Nuwaumaneetaunk
Nutaunksauag
Kutaputush Numanutoomun wuchee wamee nuwaeenuqun wuneehteawonk.
Kutaputush wuchee wamee kumagooaunash
Numanutoom
Nee naj!

Our Creator
We come unto you today
with our quiet hearts.
Thank you very much
Great Spirit in the sky for all
Our beloved
Relations
Thank you Creator for
All the beauty that surrounds us.
Thank you for all your gifts, Creator.
Be it so! (Amen)

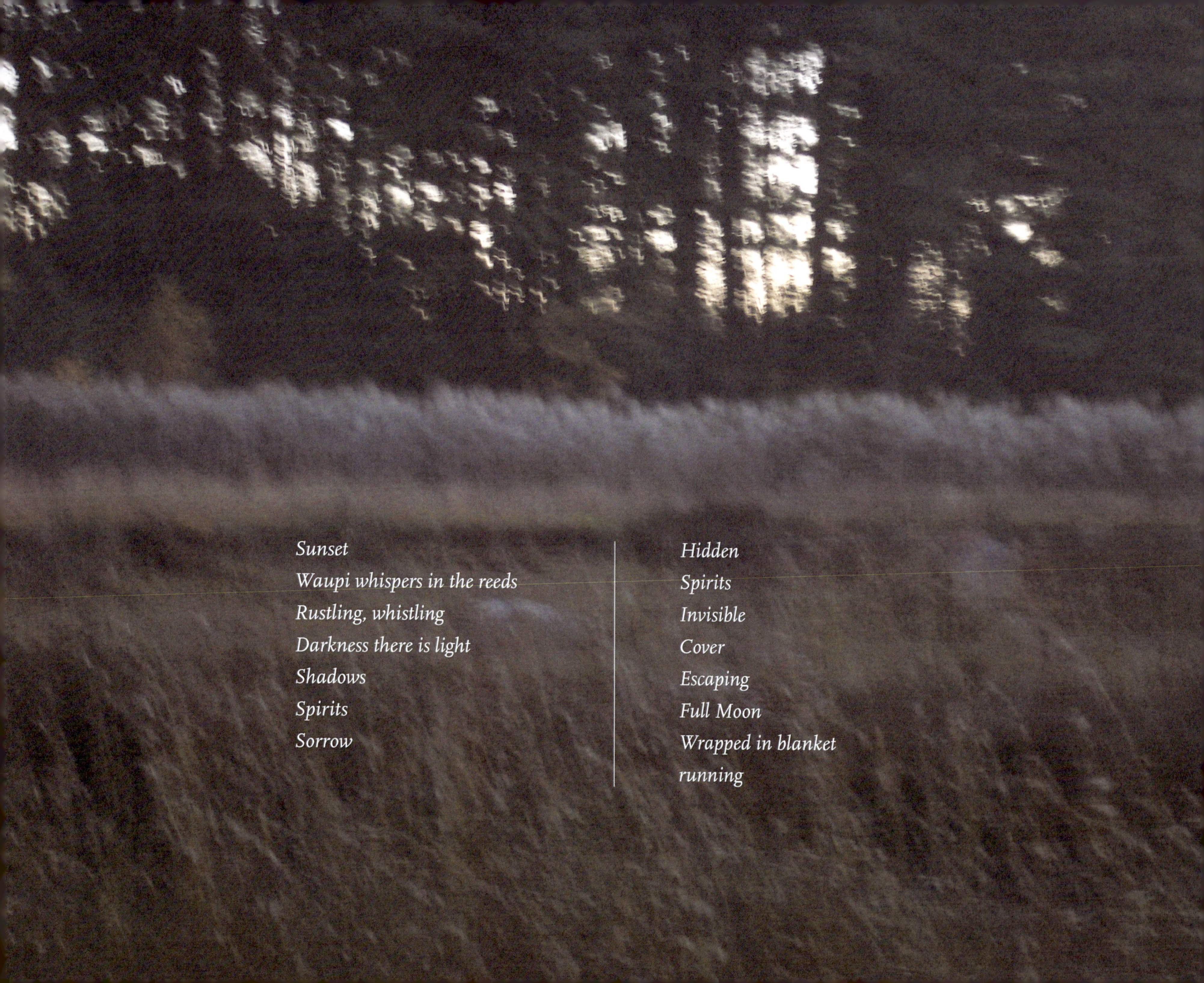

Sunset
Waupi whispers in the reeds
Rustling, whistling
Darkness there is light
Shadows
Spirits
Sorrow

Hidden
Spirits
Invisible
Cover
Escaping
Full Moon
Wrapped in blanket
running

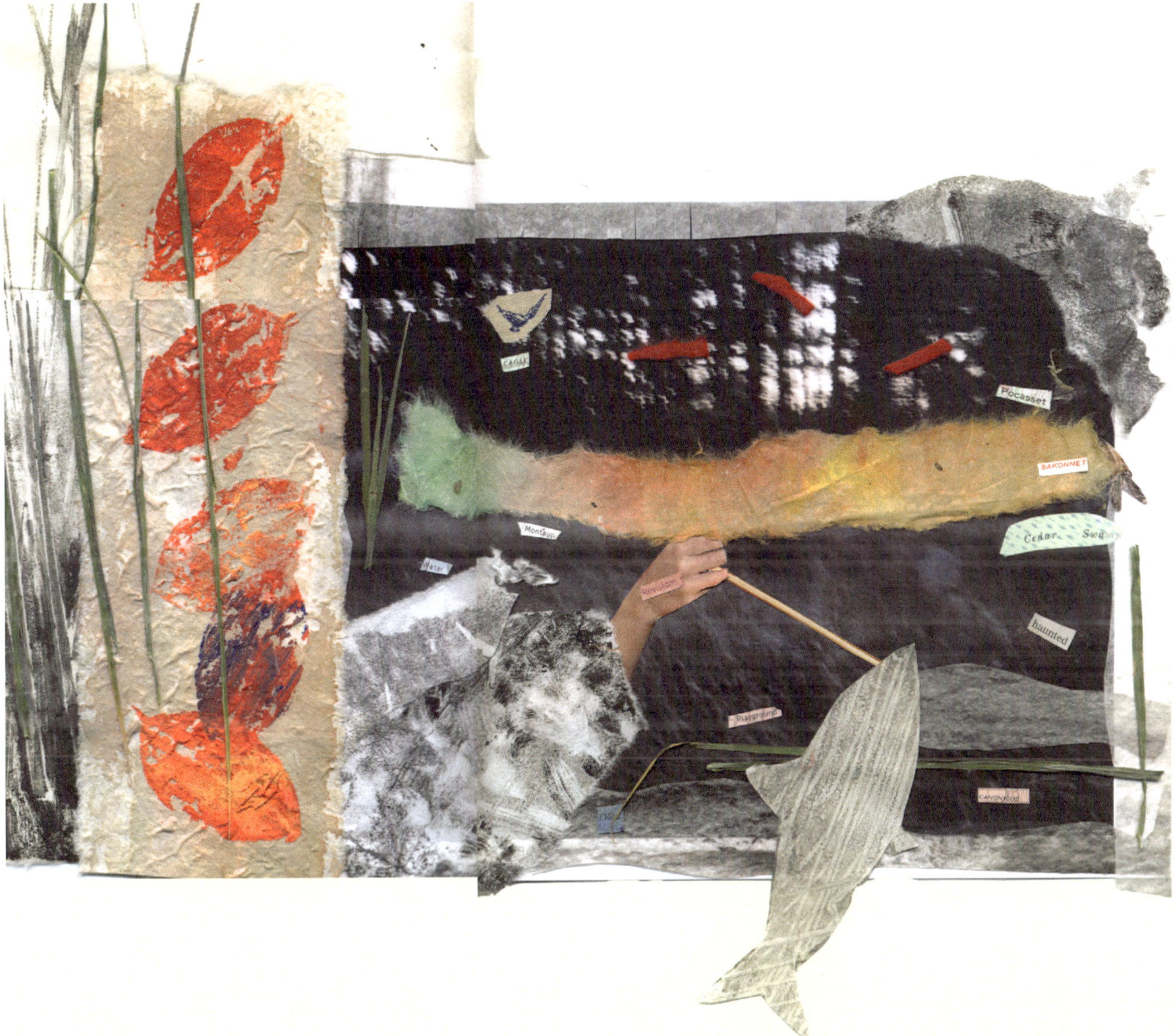

The trees weeping,
"Weta weeps"
Ancestors walk here
shadow
The waupi speaks to me
    the Ancestors are here
The light is soft
    The land is quiet
Shimmering,
    shadow
spirit, prayers, twilight, evening

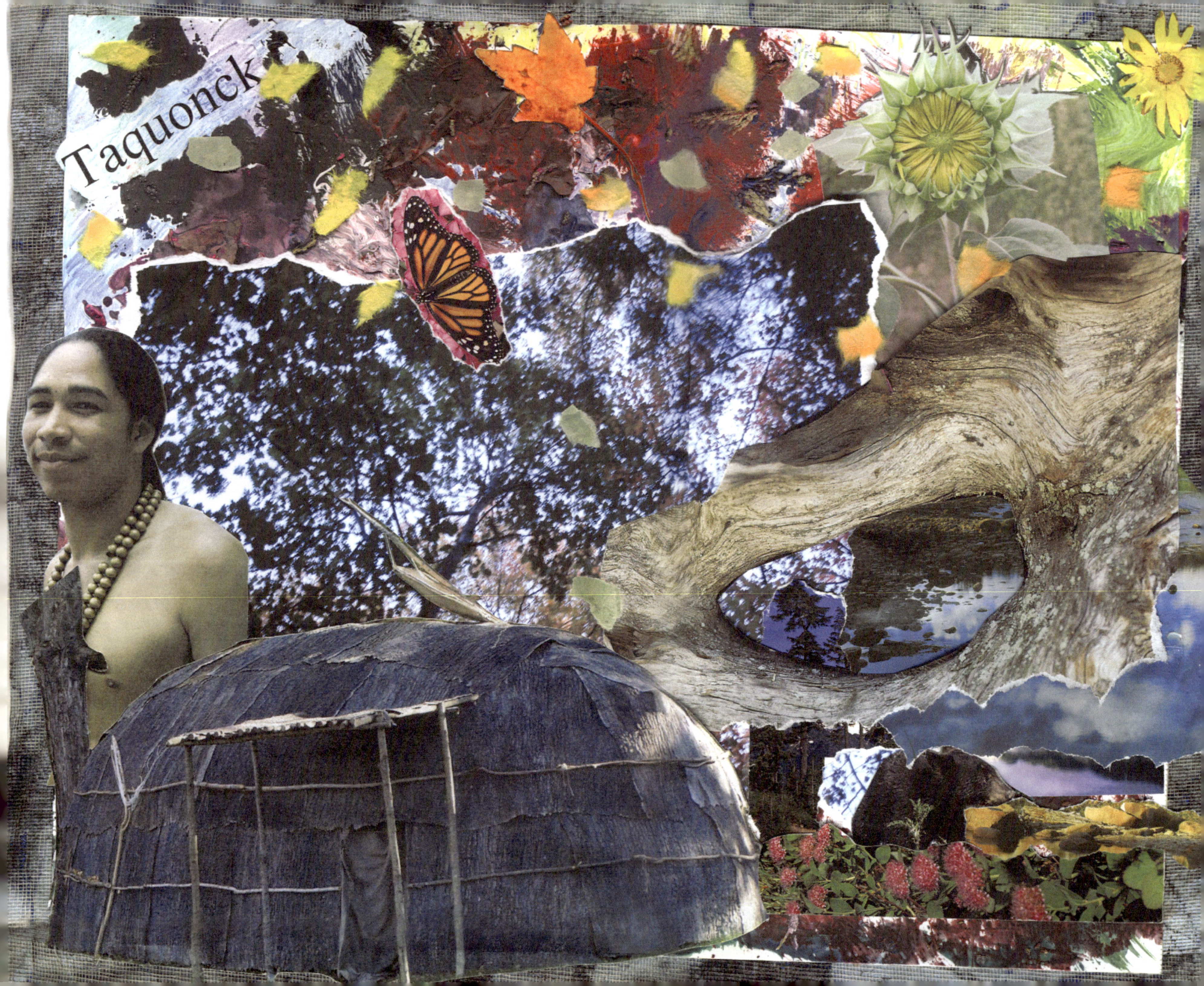
Taquonck

Mashapaug
Autumn's coming—Taquonck
Peacefulness surrounds us
Streams bring fresh water—neep.
Mashapaug
Light above
Dark below
Mashapaug

The family walks along the stream
Toward Mashapaug
They gather cranberries in their bark baskets
Tasting tart sweetness as they wander toward the sunlight.

The son spies a flowery orange mushroom.
The father is proud as he helps his young son cut it off the old oak tree.

As darkness turns to light they are startled by the cry of the osprey as he dives down to the glittering reflection of the sky in the clear water—nepewase.

Wuneeteawonk
Beauty—a weeping askashi waterfall
Ancestor's reflect the past
Spirits heal
Tranquility of heart,
Passion of mind
Healing the future.

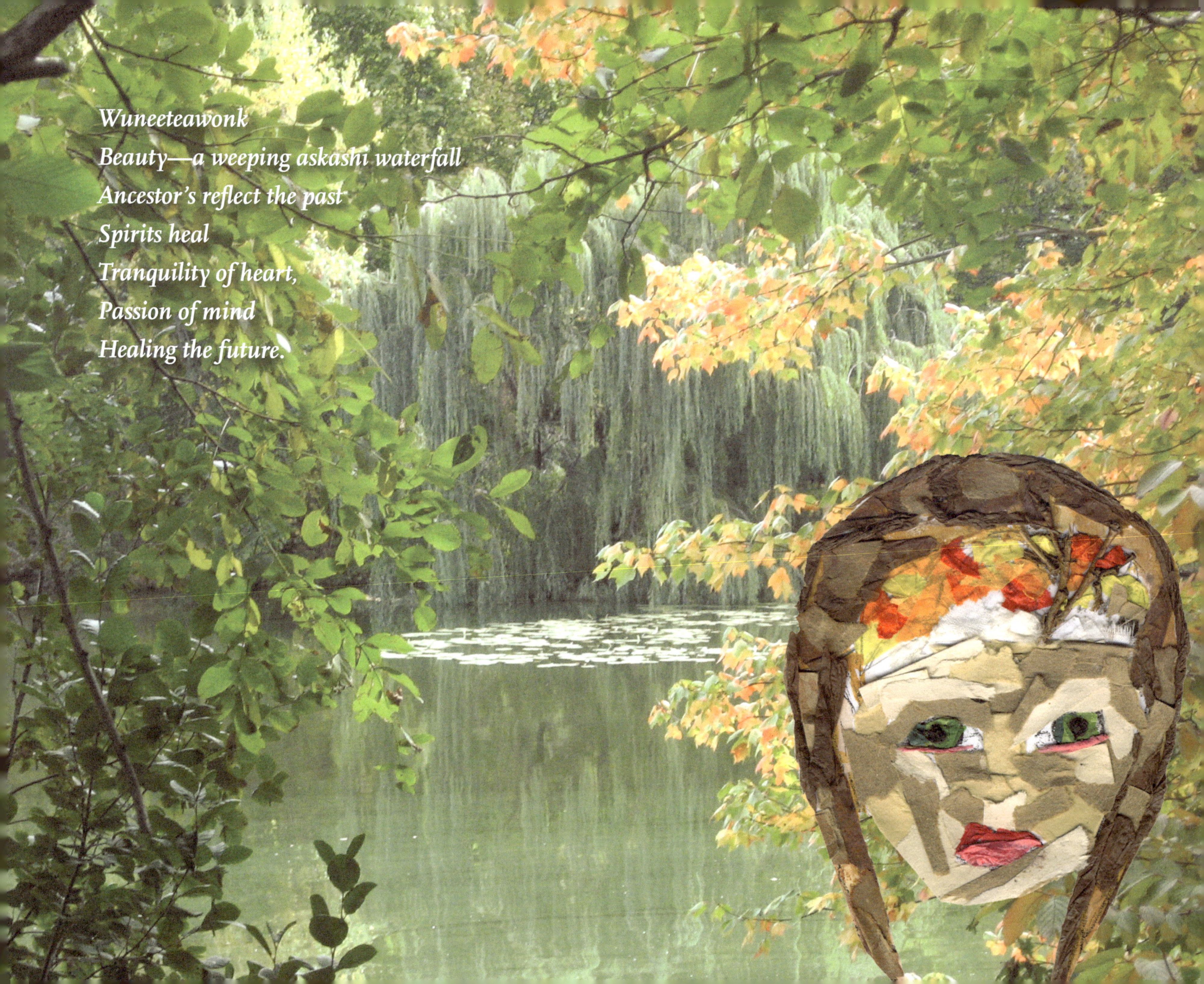

Earth lays to rest for papone
gathering, harvesting
sustaining our people

A new oak tree growing.
Dark before dawn.
New beginning waiting until Spring, Sequan.
Acorns, caps
decay, decomposition
destruction
yet we live
        we struggle, we survive
The layers of our existence
We are clay, we can remold
        ourselves—our image
        of who we are.

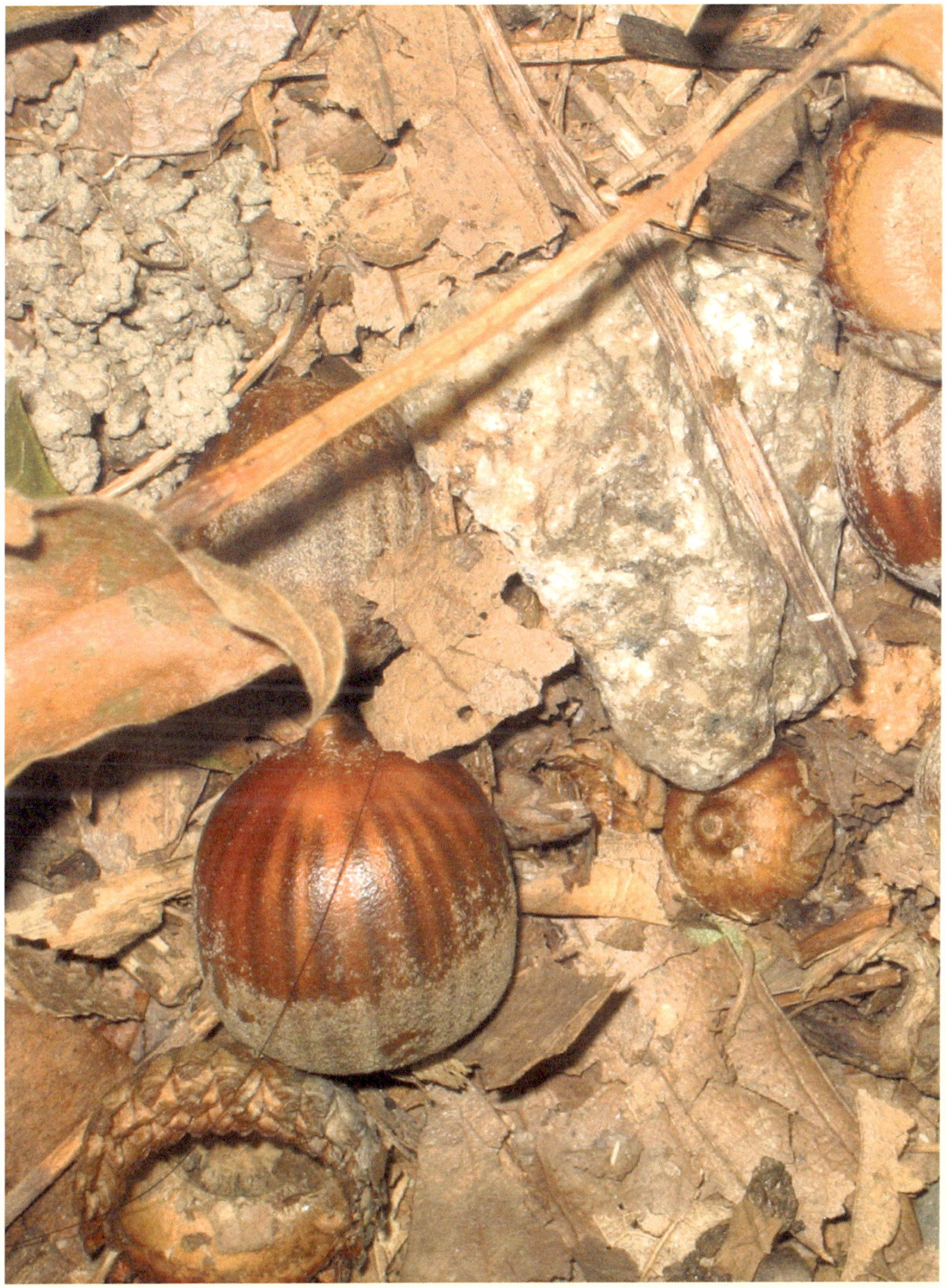

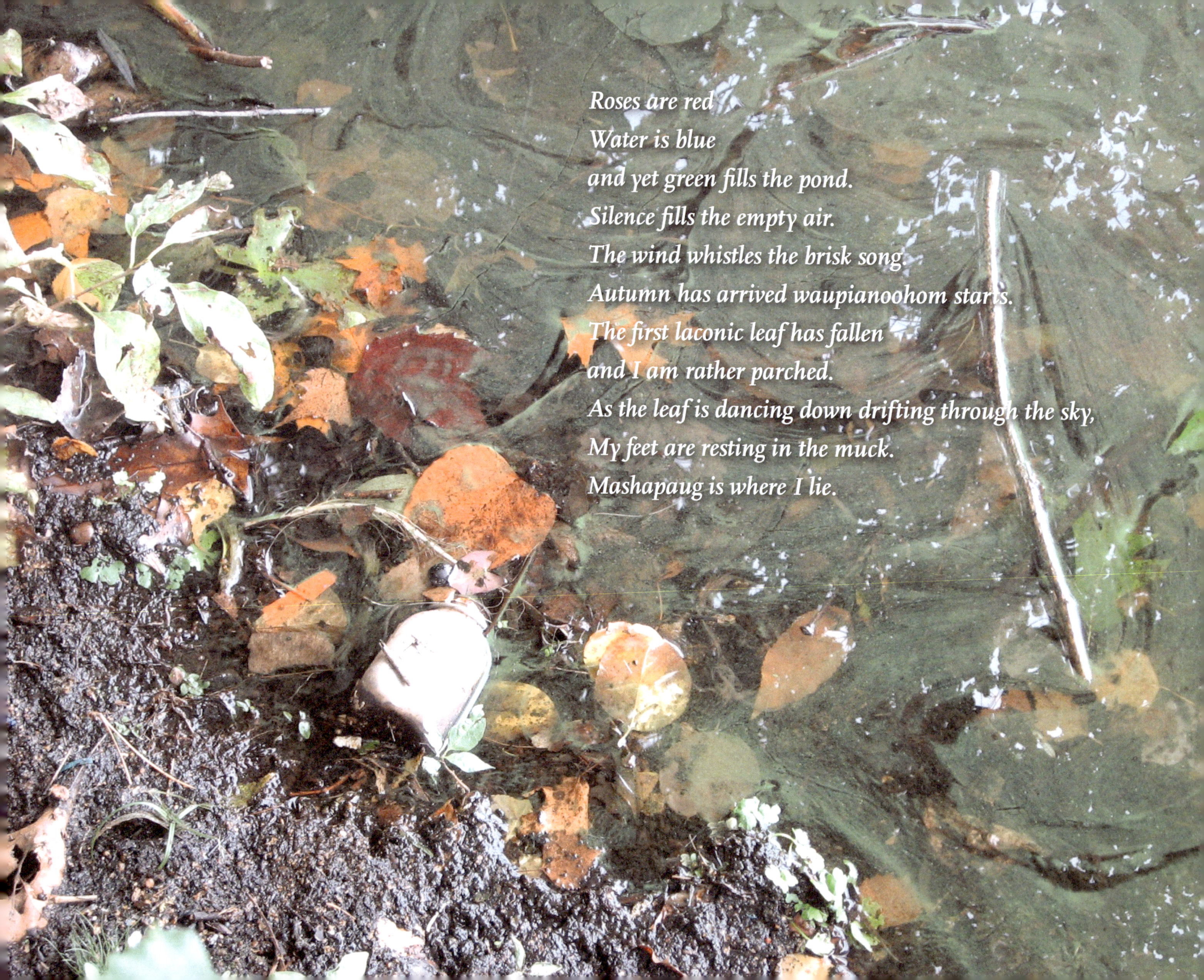

Roses are red
Water is blue
and yet green fills the pond.
Silence fills the empty air.
The wind whistles the brisk song
Autumn has arrived waupianoohom starts.
The first laconic leaf has fallen
and I am rather parched.
As the leaf is dancing down drifting through the sky,
My feet are resting in the muck.
Mashapaug is where I lie.

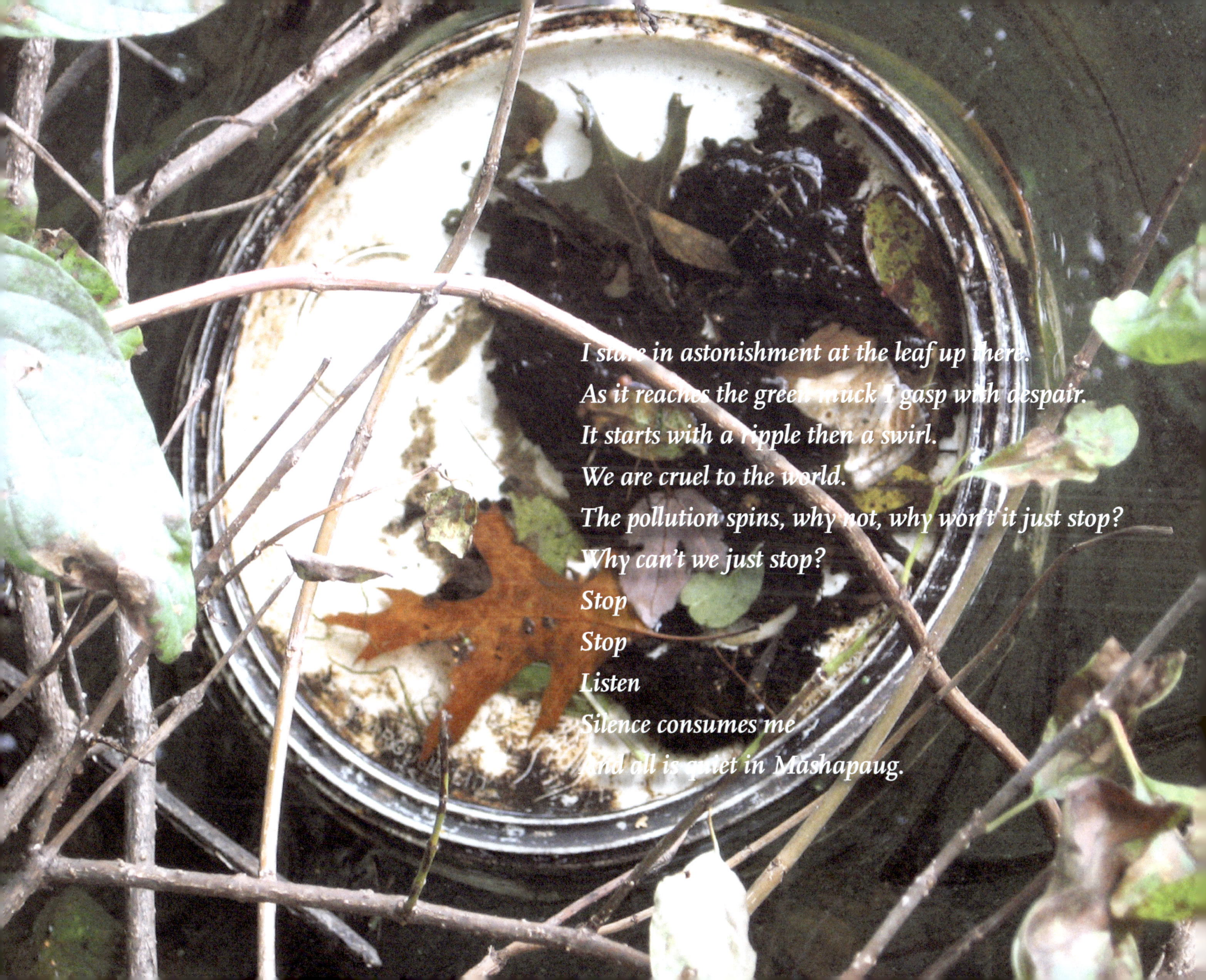

I stare in astonishment at the leaf up there.
As it reaches the green muck I gasp with despair.
It starts with a ripple then a swirl.
We are cruel to the world.
The pollution spins, why not, why won't it just stop?
Why can't we just stop?
Stop
Stop
Listen
Silence consumes me
And all is quiet in Mashapaug.

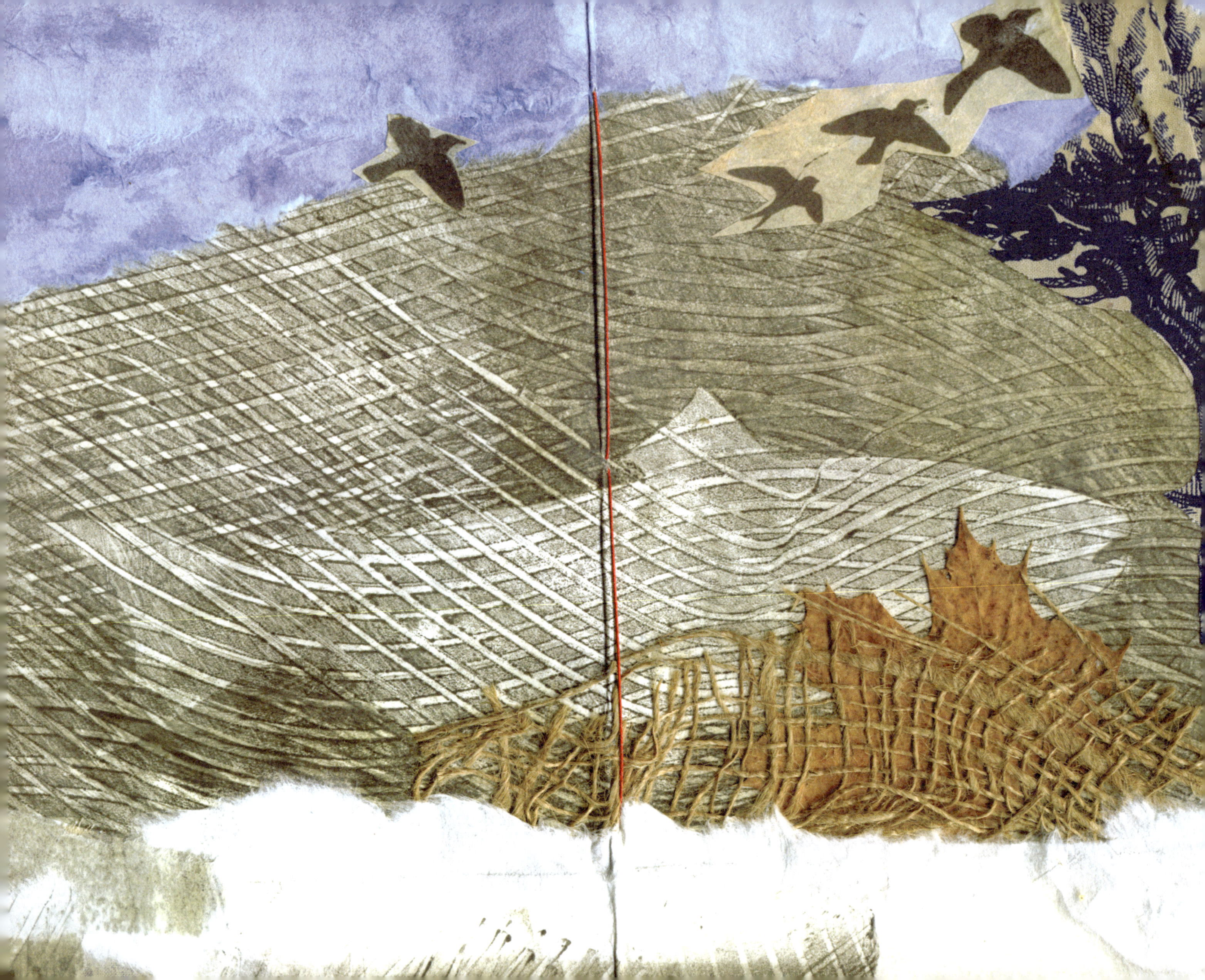

The Four Directions

Balance

We shall fly to the spirit world

The trees, they are strong and powerful

Wind washes through the trees

The trees are great with age

The sturgeon waits

The young men hunt

The weirs are set

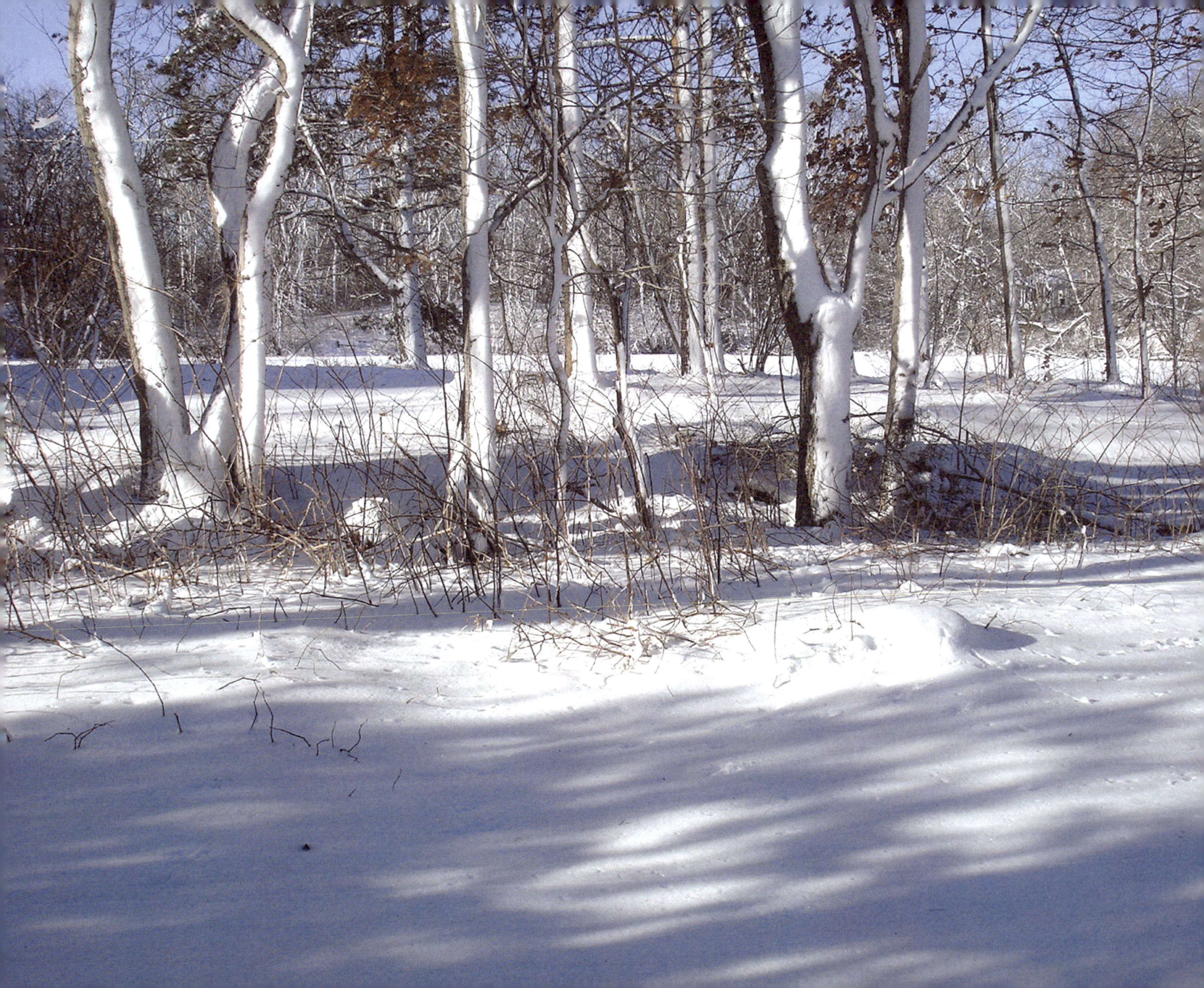

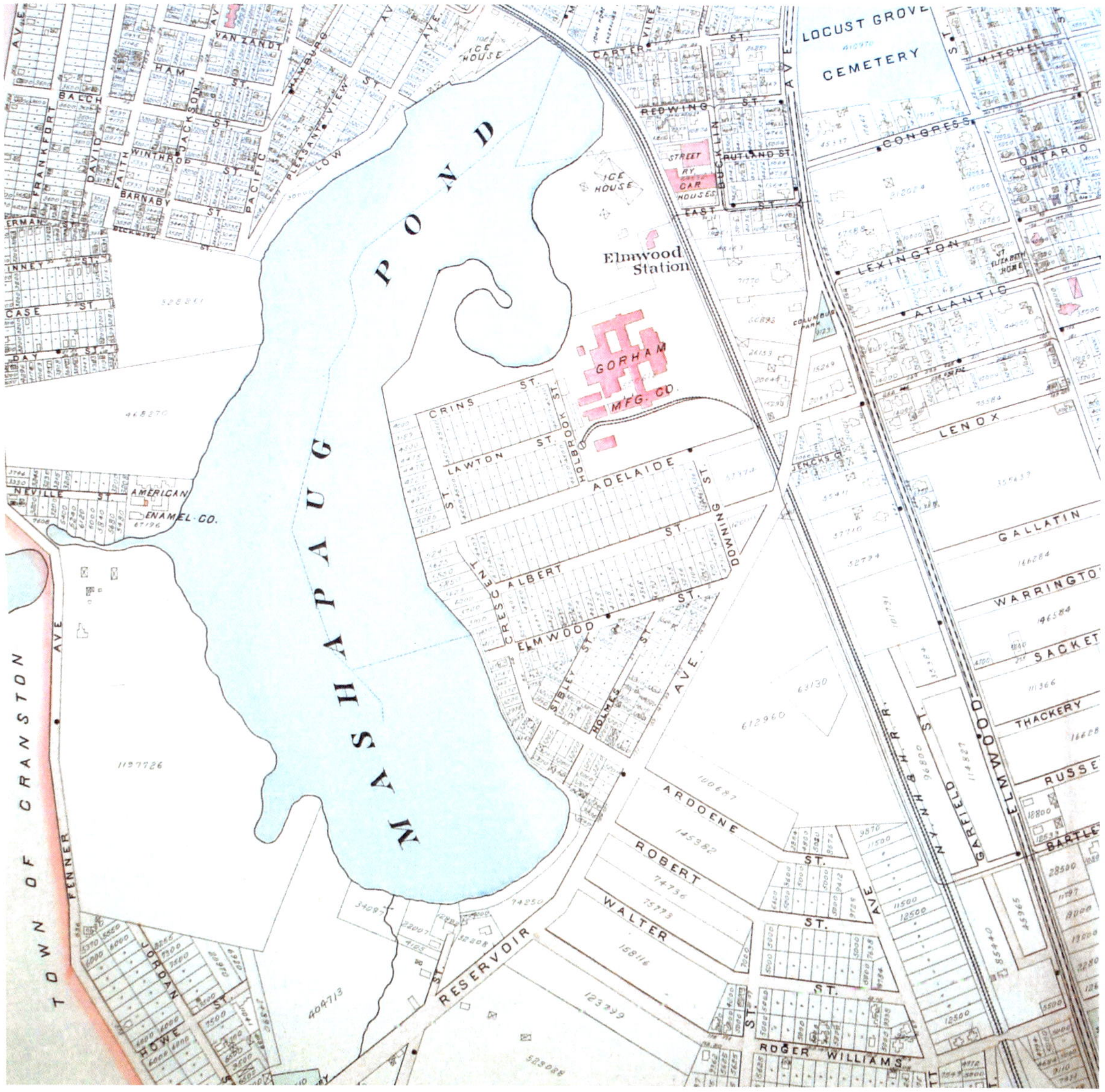
MASHAPAUG POND
LOCUST GROVE CEMETERY
GORHAM MFG. CO.
Elmwood Station
ICE HOUSE
STREET RY CAR HOUSES
AMERICAN ENAMEL CO.
TOWN OF CRANSTON
FENNER AVE
RESERVOIR
ELMWOOD
N.Y.N.H.&H.R.R.
GARFIELD
CONGRESS
ONTARIO
LEXINGTON
ATLANTIC
LENOX
GALLATIN
WARRINGTON
THACKERY
ADELAIDE
ALBERT
CRINS ST.
LAWTON ST.
DOWNING
CRESCENT
ARDOENE
ROBERT
WALTER
ROGER WILLIAMS
REDWING
RUTLAND ST.
CARTER
VAN ZANDT
HAM
BALCH
FRANKFORT
DAVID
FAITH
WINTHROP
BARNABY
PACIFIC
LOW
CASE
NEVILLE
JORDAN
HOWE

TABLE OF CONTENTS

Snow Snow Sochepwutch

Let us gather at neek—my house
Neek round—warm—together

I see the house warm and round. Look at the smile on Pummukau's face. Pummukau is only 2 winters old, yet he knows how to listen. He has the ability to listen to the family sounds. He knows the sound of nature. He sits in the warmth of the family. His face is bright in love and joy. The warmth of the fire comforts the family. Pummukau's father is telling the family stories. Stories are told during the winter months.

Snow has fallen
The people are warm in their homes
The old ones tell the stories
The stories of the times of the Spirit Beings
Snow has fallen on our lands.

Snow on the ground
At dawn father out tracking the deer
He gets one!
It is tied to a limb, hanging from a sturdy tree.
I am thinking how wonderful it is to have venison.

Sochepo
Jumping in the snow
Lots of footprints, like rabbits
Wood sleds that go down are pulled up
snowflakes
More snowflakes and the hills
People are in their long houses
lighting the fire
opening the smoke holes
sitting on the wooden benches
Eating

THE WISDOM OF THE EAGLE SPEAKS TO US

Many people have walked this land. We have seen Mashapaug full of life and change. Deer and humans have left their mark, but the mark of the deer does not last long. Man's greed endangers all of our future. The toxic chemicals dumped into Mashapaug poison us still. The Silver industry has gone but its toxic effects linger and cause harm to all life. The people must learn to protect Noohkasahkee.

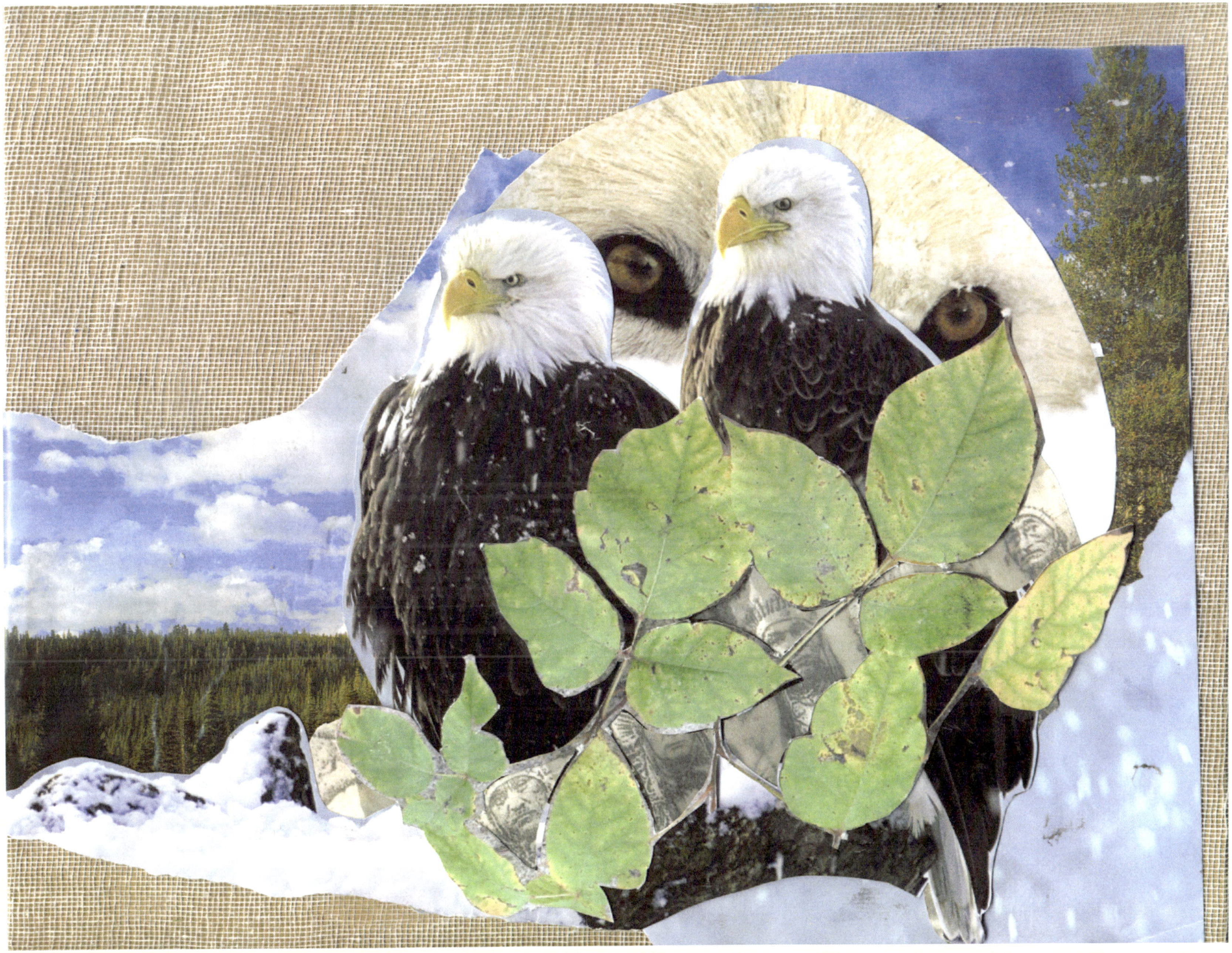

Home,
the place of the Ancestors
Layers of usurpation—seen
as street upon street
pollution upon pollution.
How have you taken so much
when you have cared
so little.
The people cry

Twilight's Hour
Time to contemplate
The future

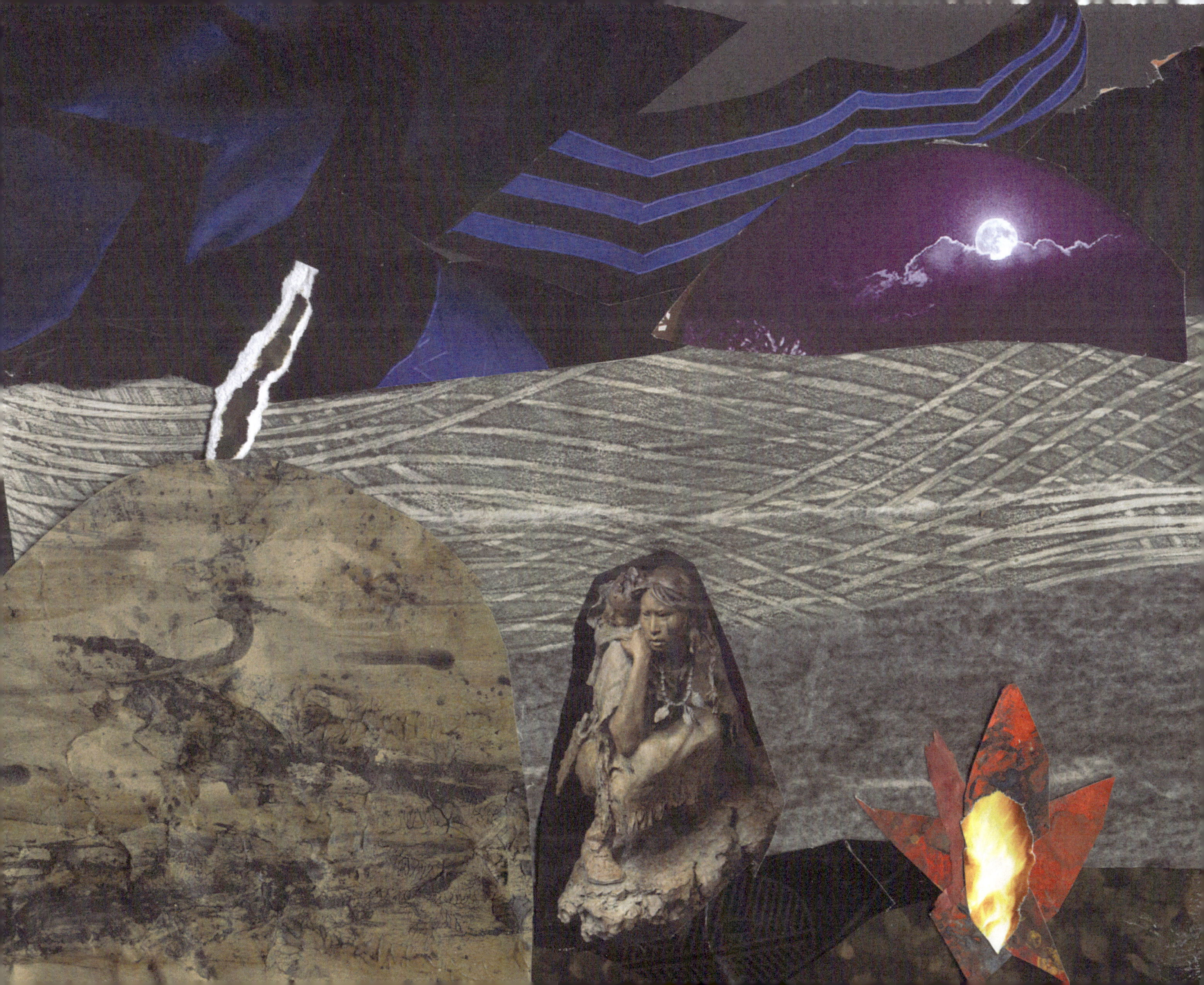

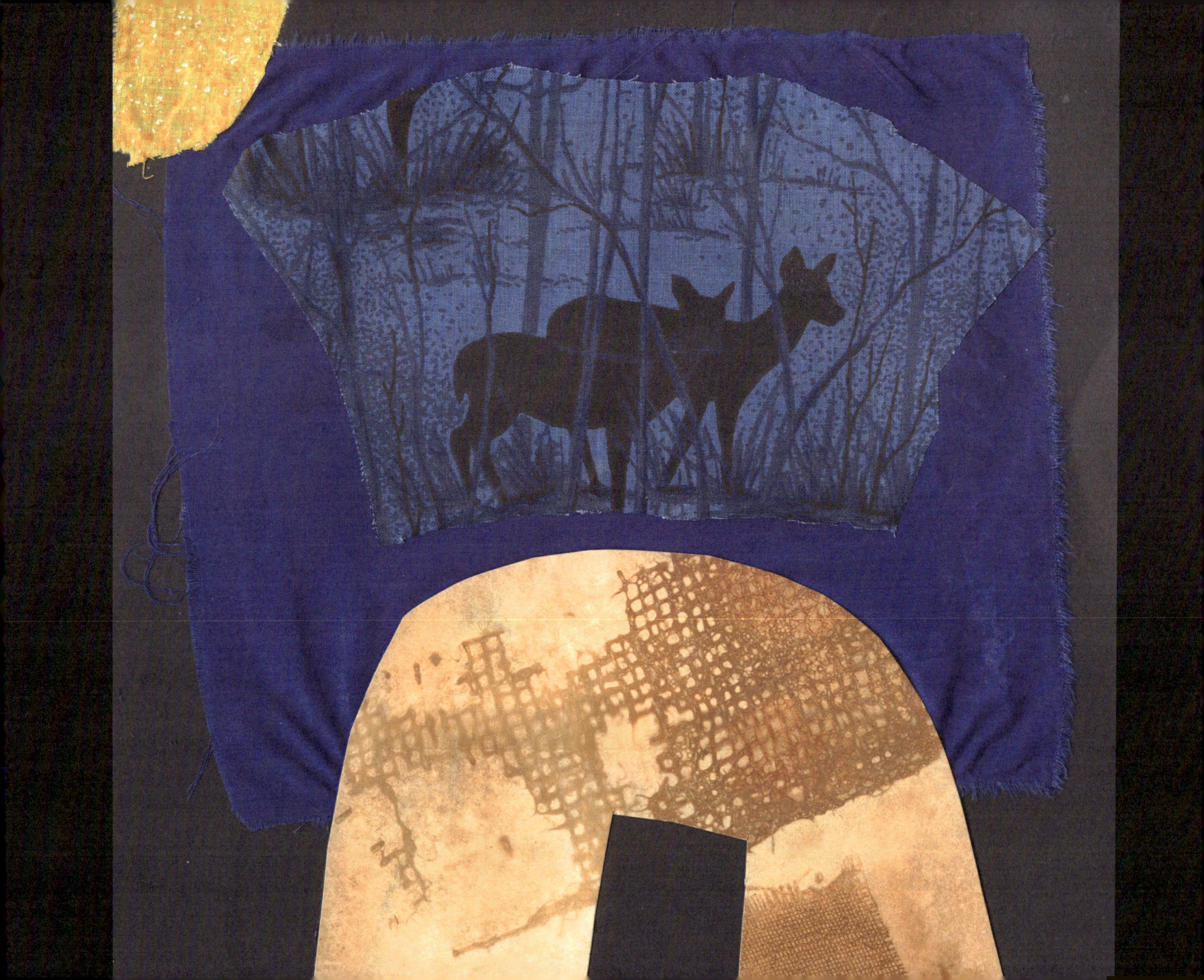

I see deer
I smell different trees
Blue and black.
small house
fire smoke
memory
spirits/spiritual
liquid/swirling
patterns
celestial

Nanepashet is shining on the
ahtuquag.
We are safe.
Feel the warmth of the fire in the wetu.
I feel desperation,
Grandmother

Nukomis Nanepashet watches over the night
We travel by her light—weqai!
Our home is safe
The beauty of the mats of the wetu
help me have beautiful dreams
I am surrounded by beauty
I am safe in the swamp
The bark covering keeps out the cold wind
Stay close to me.

Indigenous life in Rhode Island, an introduction

By Paulla Dove Jennings as told to Holly Ewald with artwork by Nkéke and Sherenté Harris

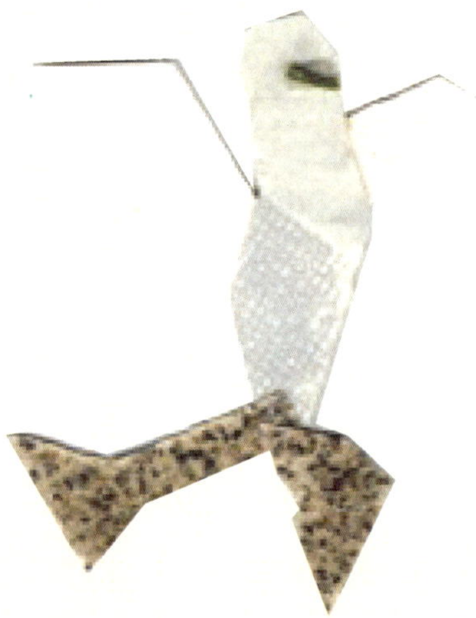

During the summer of 2010, I interviewed Paulla Dove Jennings, a Narragansett/Niantic Elder who was raised in the Narragansett community. She has devoted her life to educating people regarding the history and culture of the Narragansett Nation. I asked her to describe how her ancestors might have lived on Mashapaug Pond before 1636, when Europeans settled in Providence. I originally organized this material to prepare Urban Pond Procession teaching artists to help students envision how this sustainable culture lived around their local pond prior to 1600. It is my hope, as well the hope of the elders who created this book, that other teachers can use this information to educate Rhode Island students about Narragansett culture.

Paulla often explained the history she knew through oral history and stories. She moved back and forth through time, talking about settlements around Mashapaug Pond in the past and ways of living today that maintain and reflect cultural traditions.

Paulla grew up without electricity until age nine in Charlestown, Rhode Island, on Buckeye Brook Trail. She bathed in a spring. Her family might have eaten jonnycakes four nights a week with whatever fish or shellfish had been gathered that day. Jonnycakes are a food that has been passed down from long ago and continue to be a Rhode Island staple. Jonnycakes are made from white flint cornmeal and were traditionally cooked on hot stones.

Though her family was poor, she never felt poor because there was a great deal of fun and laughter in their home. At night her family members played guitar, read books; they sang, learned songs, and told stories, sometimes scary stories. The gathering of family to feast followed by music, storytelling, and games are the same types of things that happened four or five hundred years ago. "It was all a learning experience, everything was there for a reason. It was not only learning but it was sharing and laughter and having fun."

She told a story about waiting by a large rock set on a ledge for the school bus when she was in elementary school. One day her father showed her that there were three small rocks at its base. He removed the rocks and moved the large rock back and forth. She could move it, too, even though it was huge. The sound could be heard for miles. It is called a 'cup and saucer rock' or 'drum rock' and was used by the Narragansett to communicate over long distances. The sacred talking rocks can be found all along the eastern seaboard still today.

When she was three months old, Paulla was given the name Sunflower by Chief Strong Horse. She disliked her name until she read an autobiography her daughter, Little Fawn, wrote for a college class. Little Fawn was grieving because her brother had died and she recalled being comforted by her mother. She knew she could turn to Paulla because she stood tall, with her head up, smiling just like her name, Sunflower. So Paula grew into her name, and realized its gift.

Narragansett Settlements: When the English first came to this land, the Narragansett were the largest and strongest tribe in what is now called Southern New England. Narragansett Territory spanned most of what is now Rhode Island connected into Connecticut and Massachusetts. The territory bordered with the Niantic to the south, the Wampanoag in the east, the Nipmuk to the north, tribute tribes, and the Pequod to the west. There were a number of Narragansett communities throughout Rhode Island, many of which settled around ponds such as Mashapaug.

In the summer the Indigenous People located mostly by the shore, living in weetus. A weetu ("WEE too") is a temporary circular dome-shaped home with a frame made of bent saplings covered with mats made of cattails tied together and attached to the frame. In the winter, families moved inland and lived together in shwísh-quttow (house of three fires) or longhouses, which were large dwellings that accommodated from five to twenty families. Each family had their own section. Longhouses were made similarly to the weetu but were long and rectangular with domed half circle ends and several smoke holes. Bark was used instead of cattails for the covering with beautiful woven interior mats or wall hangings called mannotaúbana. Since it is only about three miles from the coast, Mashapaug was quite possibly both a winter and summer settlement.

In the spring the women and girls gathered cattails and bulrushes for the weetus. The bulrushes were woven into waterproof mats, which had many uses inside the homes including wall hangings, bed coverings, and seating. These mats stayed with the family as it moved back and forth from summer home to winter home. In the summer homes, the cooking was done outside and the water left in the bulrushes cooled the inside of the weetu. In the winter longhouses, the fires inside heated the water in the bullrushes creating steam heat adding warmth and comfort to the shelter.

Summer Settlements: Each family had its own garden and weetu; women and girls would tend the gardens. They grew corn, beans, squash, cucumbers, melons, and sunflowers. Summer gardens were prepared at both Mashapaug and at the summer settlements nearer the shore. As they worked, mothers would tell stories to teach their daughters about Mother Earth and Father Sky. In the spring and fall, men and boys fished buckeyes (alewives) and shad (river herring). Fish came up Mashapaug Brook along with Atlantic salmon who were spawning their eggs in the fresh water. The Narragansett dried and smoked fish, game, and other foods for winter.

They didn't raise livestock; the Indigenous People hunted for their meat, and shellfish and fish were an important part of their diet. They didn't add salt to their food. They seafood they ate supplied with the salt their bodies needed. Sweets were found in berries and maple syrup.

"When the leaves on the maple tree are the size of a field mouse's ear then you knew the sap was getting ready to run and then you would start to tap the trees and gather the sap. And actually I like the sap directly out of the tree. It's not sweet like when it boils down, but it has a nice, soothing taste; I like it chilled," Paulla explained.

Winter Settlements: Winter settlements were built inland on high ground where a number of families, related on their mother's side, would live in one longhouse. The longhouse area was surrounded by closely placed wooden stakes called 'palisades' which protected people from the weather and animals. In pre-contact times there were bears, wolves, and big cats (or catamounts) as well as deer, moose, elk, and a few wood bison. White turkeys that had black tips on their feathers called Narragansett turkeys lived along the coast. On Mashapaug Pond, Narragansett would have fed themselves by ice fishing and hunting and trapping.

The longhouses were laid in relationship with each other and with respect to the lay of the land, with one meetinghouse large enough to accommodate everyone. Sometimes another community would be invited to decide boundaries for hunting and planting. They worked together as a whole, sitting and planning.

Winter activities: Winter was a time for gaining knowledge that could be used and built on during the summer. Drumming, songs, and the different rhythms of the rattles were taught in the winter. The traditional drumbeat represents the heartbeat of Mother Earth. 1,2 - 1,2 - 1,2 - 1,2. The honor beats were stronger. "They became a louder and more distinctive in their rhythm. Dancers recognize them immediately and one can see the shift in the dancers' movements," Paulla explained. "They are honoring the gifts given by the Creator." At the Powwows and socials today, when Indigenous People hear the honor beats, they do something special in recognition. Fir example, the young girls and women might hold their fans high in the air; the boys and men might do a distinctive dance step. In the winter you also would learn about the thirteen different thanksgivings. At each new moon there was something to give thanks for; for example, thanksgivings celebrate the maple syrup, the green corn, the strawberry, and the cranberry. Everyone would put in whatever food they had available to share with others on these occasions. In the winter the Narragansett played many games of chance. People used the products of their best skills, such as basket making, tanning, or knife making, to compete and gamble. Feasting, gaming, singing, and storytelling were all part of winter gatherings.

Education: Learning was ongoing. Throughout the interview Paulla emphasized the role of the elders as the educators who imparted knowledge through storytelling and oral history. "There would be a time at the pond where they told the stories and the history of the people and that would be the most important thing because the children would learn through them," she explained. Children might look at feathers and group them in terms of size or color. They would think of uses for the feathers. They would learn to identify the birds by their feathers and appreciate the gifts from the Creator.

All children learned to swim in ponds, in preparation for swimming in the ocean. They learned about the world around them through exploration. The child learned by following the example of the older children and adults.

Discipline was taught to children by giving them questions to encourage them to think about their actions. Mostly stories were told to teach children the morals and values of the community.

Games: In the Moccasin game three moccasins were set up with a stone in one of them. The moccasins were moved around and the other player picked which one had the stone.

Football was played at the shore near the summer homes. A football was made by layering grasses and leather until it was a "decent size ball." A small arbor was built where people put what they wanted to gamble, such as baskets, tools, skins, or fishing nets. The football goals were usually two or three miles apart and games usually lasted for three days and two nights. The first day a pit was built in which seafood, root potatoes, corn, green onions, clams, lobsters, and crabs were cooked for feasting during the game. The pits were lined with stones and heated. Kelp covered the food and kept it moist as it steamed. Today the Narragansett continue to play these and other traditional games known as hub-bub, hand-game, ring and pin, lacrosse, and fireball. Games are used in ceremony for healing, for socialization and fun, and as a means of barter.

Girls: Women were leaders, sachems, and warriors, and even today there are women on the Tribal Council. They were taught the importance of the gift the Creator gave to them, to be the givers of life. Girls usually tended the gardens with their mothers who also taught them about the various dyes from berries, roots, or bark and how to scrape and tan skins as well as to weave ash splint baskets, quilt, and bead. The mothers told stories about how the plants came to be there and their medicinal uses. They would learn which herbs to gather and how to use them for teas or for medicinal compresses, how to collect seeds for the following spring. Seeds were stored in a cool stone-lined hole in the ground. The innards of milkweed were padded together and used for diapers. Elders told stories while the girls learned to weave their first baskets. They learned to paint plant designs on baskets. The youngest girls learned how to twist the grasses together to make short pieces of twine. The eight-to-ten-year-old girls put the small pieces together to make long strings of twine and the oldest learned how to make nets out of the twine, which might be used for fishing weirs.

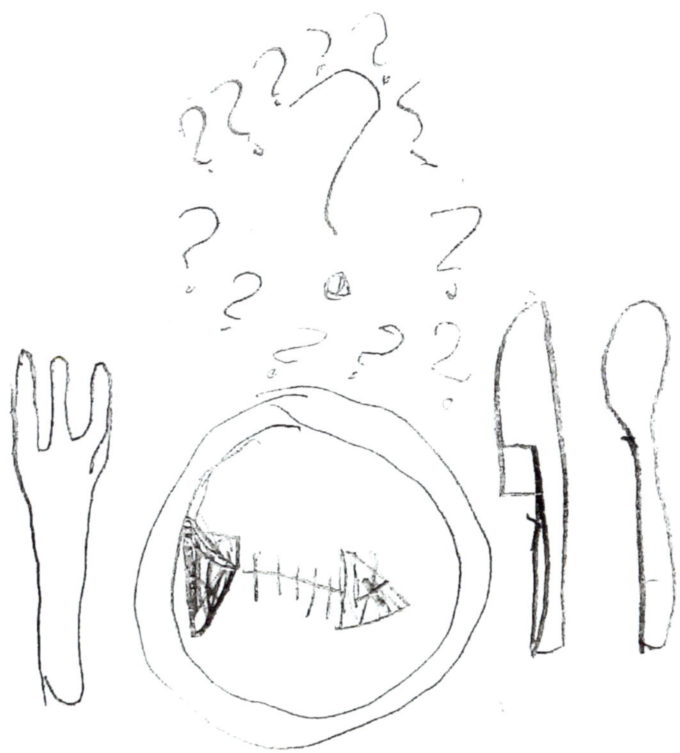

Boys: Boys were taught to work with stone, which included shaping stones for fishing weights and making spears for spring spearfishing in Mashapaug Brook. They shaped rocks to scrape the fish and skins, and they made pounding stones to do the shaping. Boys often built tall stands in the gardens where they watched for birds and small animals, such as rabbits and woodchucks, feeding off the plants. They scared the birds and animals away with slingshots. They also used tools to make animal traps, fish weirs, canoe paddles, and dugout canoes, the largest of which could hold up to forty people. Once felled, the tree for the dugout canoe would be lit on fire and the charred wood scraped, burned again, scraped, burned, scraped until it was hollowed out enough for the men to sit inside. Once a year they went whaling. One whale was shared by many communities.

When the men and boys went out fishing or hunting, elders often told stories about other hunts and how to use all parts of the animals. The sinew from the deer might be used to bind things together, its hide scraped clean for clothing, its meat cooked or dried for food, and its hoofs and nose boiled down for glue to waterproof an object. They learned "to take," as Paulla said instead of "to kill," only what they needed when they went hunting. They were told not to take the first deer, especially if it was a doe. They also might hear creation stories such as how the deer came to be.

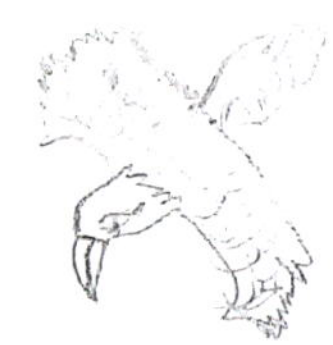

Older boys had more responsibilities. They learned to take the first fish home either to family or to an elder or someone who was sick. They were learning to be part of the community and strengthening the community.

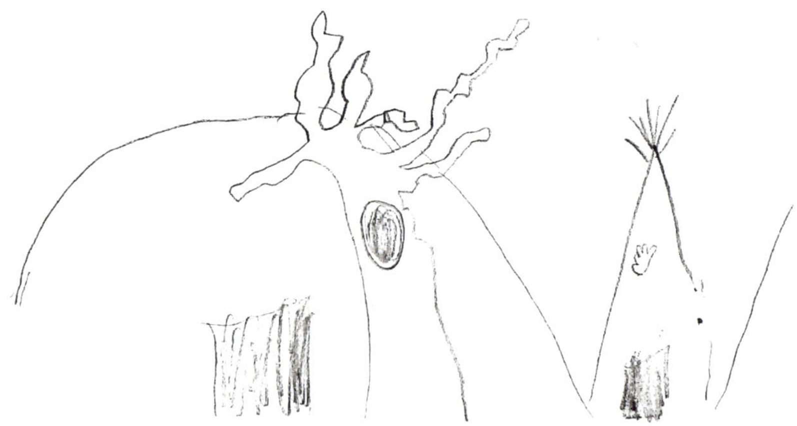

Sachems: Sachems are leaders who must protect the people and ensure their survival. The sachem moved among different groups to work out any disagreements. Other groups such as the Niantic paid tribute in the form of food or tools to the Narragansett sachem in exchange for protection from other communities. These gifts were to be given away to the sachem's people. Mashapaug Pond, as well as the place now called College Hill, were very possibly important meeting places. They each have natural amphitheaters, which could accommodate hundreds of people.

Today the sachem is elected for a six-year term according to tribal by-laws and election codes. Previously the sachem was an earned position. In addition to a supreme sachem of the whole nation there were sub-chiefs who led each village. In April 1983, the Narragansett Indian Tribe, a Sovereign Nation, became a Federally Acknowledged Tribe.

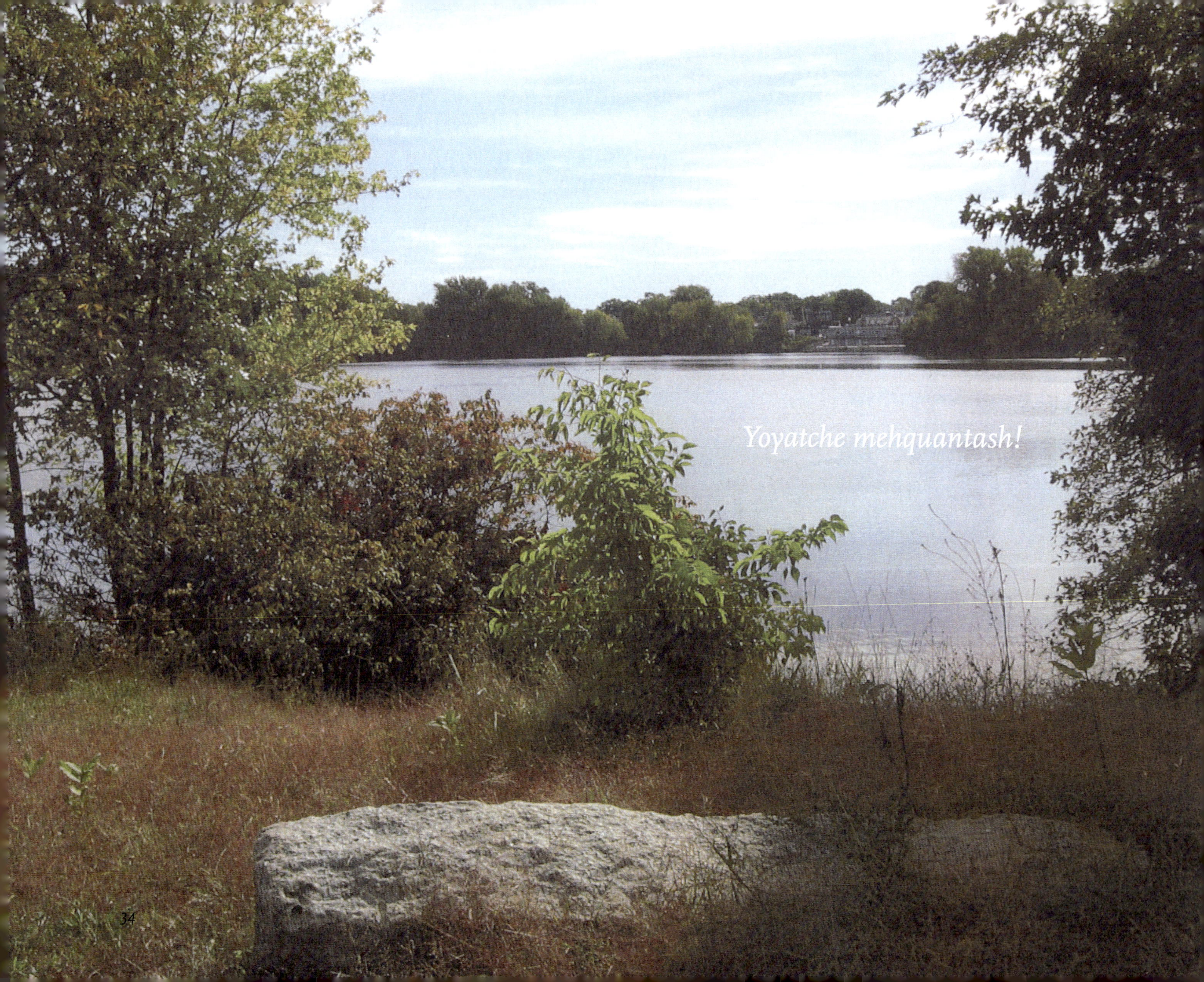

Yoyatche mehquantash!

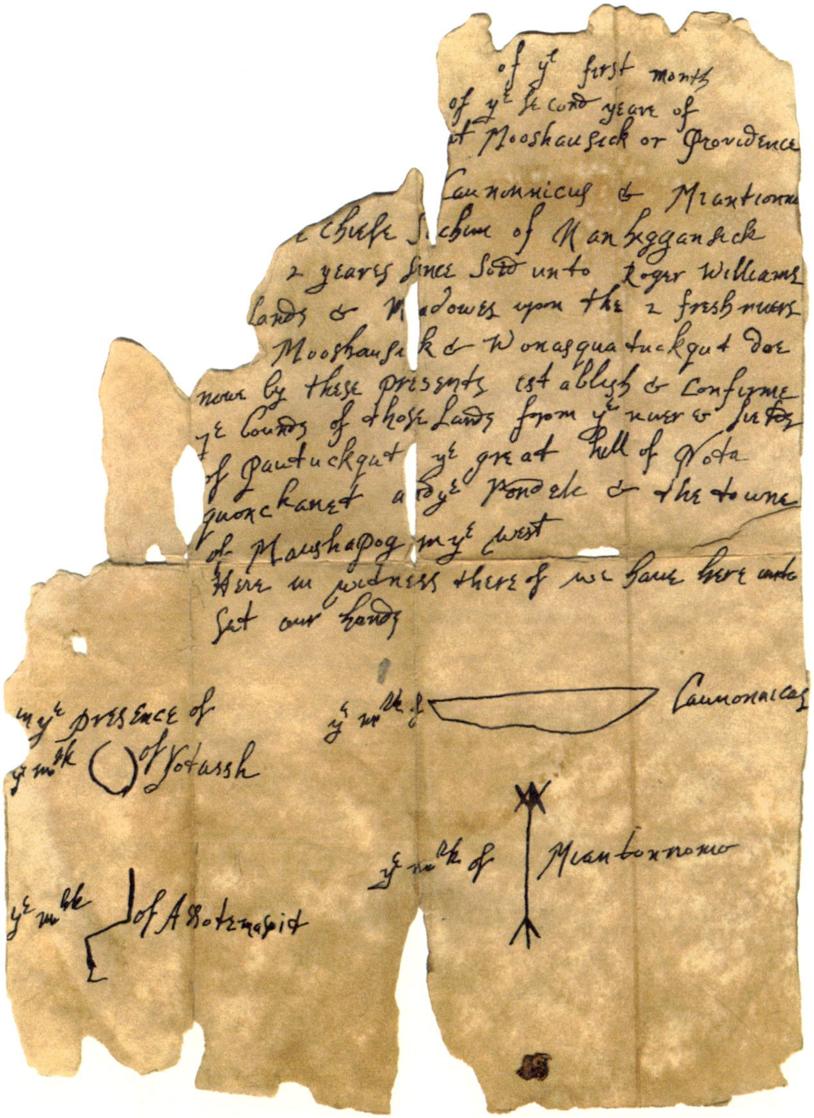

Facsimile of original agreement between Miantonomi and Roger Williams siting Mashapaug Pond, courtesy John McNiff, Roger Williams National Memorial.

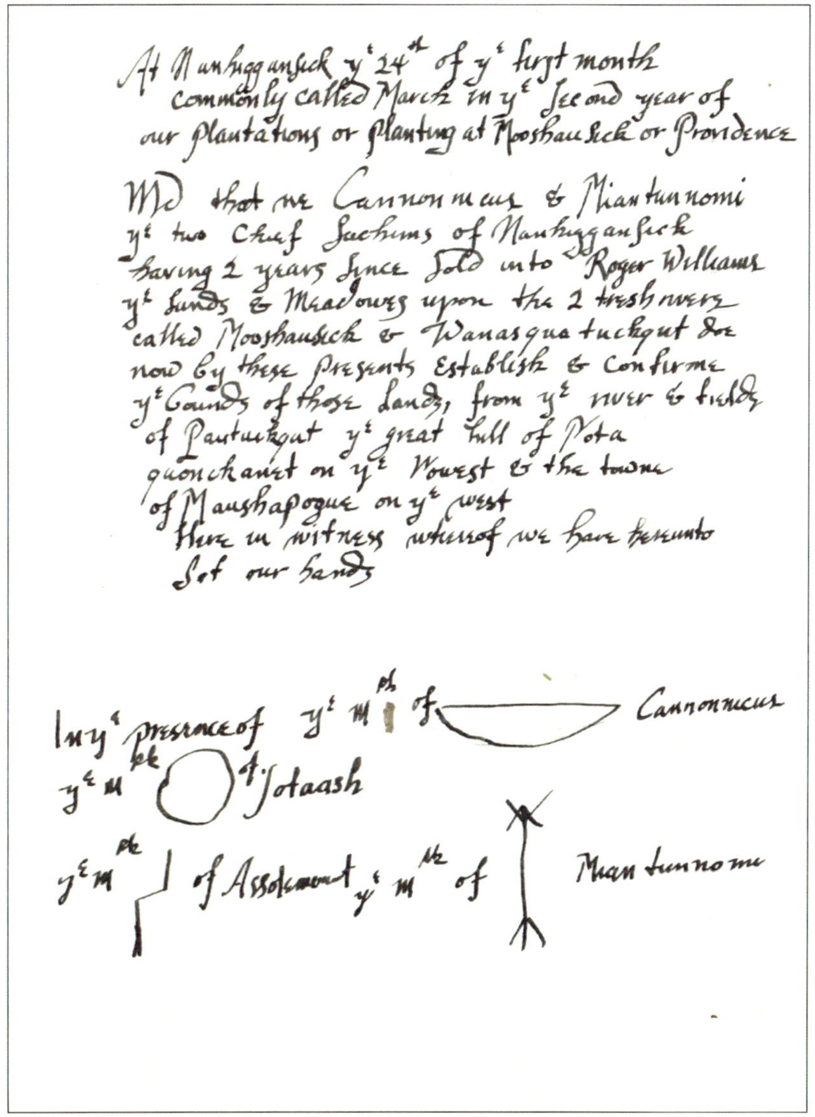

At Nanhiggansick ye 24th of ye first month
commonly called March in ye second year of
our Plantations or planting at Mooshausick or Providence

Md that we Cannonnicus & Miantunnomi
ye two Chief Sachims of Nanhiggansick
having 2 years since sold unto Roger Williams
ye lands & Meadowes upon the 2 fresh rivers
called Mooshausick & Wanasquatucket doe
now by these presents Establish & Confirme
ye bounds of those lands, from ye river & fields
of Pautuckqut ye great hill of Nota
quonckanet on ye Norwest & the towne
of Maushapogue on ye west
Here in witness whereof we have hereunto
Set our hands

In ye presence of ye mark of Cannonnicus
ye mark of Jotaash
ye mark of Assotemewit ye mark of Miantunnomi

Original agreement clarified by John McNiff, Roger Williams National Memorial.

The Continuous Presence of Native People at Mashapaug Pond

Dr. William Simmons, *Anthropology Professor at Brown University*
Transcribed from a talk given at the Tomaquag Indian Memorial Museum, 12/15/10, with artwork by Sherenté Harris

The Narragansett were the largest language group in Rhode Island and their boundary more or less coincided with the boundaries of Rhode Island. The Narragansett and the groups affiliated with the Narragansett lived in concentrations all over the state of Rhode Island. One of those places where they were very heavily concentrated was in that area that is now the west end of Providence, the West Elmwood district and the Arlington section of Cranston, Potters Avenue, that whole area. As you may know there is a series of ponds in that part of Providence. There's Spectacle Pond which is, the pond you see when you look out the window of the Twin Oaks Restaurant. Not too far from there is another little pond called Tongue Pond which is the place where the Narragansett Brewery, like Gorham Manufacturing, dumped all of its manufacturing materials. And then there's the very large pond, the biggest of them all and that's Mashapaug which is bounded by Niantic Ave., Reservoir Ave., maybe Public Street, and then the Cranston boundary to the north.

Interestingly there were two other ponds in that same area. If you know where Gilbert Stuart Middle School is, in back of that middle school there is a very large playground, baseball park, and what now is called Bucklin Park. That was a pond, called Long Pond. It was filled in. In addition to Long Pond there was another one between Cranston Street and Webster Avenue by the railroad tracks. That area may look like it was an old sand and a gravel pit, great basin in the ground. It was at one point filled with water; that was known as Benedict Pond. And those five ponds basically were the area where large numbers of Narragansett-related groups had their summer and their winter residency.

And how long did they live there? Ah, it's hard to say. But we know there have been people in the northeastern part of the United States back about 15-17 thousand years. So we can assume that people were living in those parts of Rhode Island as early as that. And I know for sure archeological pieces have been found. To my knowledge there has been no systematic archeology done on the Mashapaug Pond area. I know from the point of view of finds that people have made, various artifacts that people have found over the years, that it is a pretty sure thing that Narragansetts were living there at the time of the Colonial Historical period. They had ancestors that were living three, four, five thousand years ago for sure. So it has been inhabited for a long, long time.

When the English arrived in Providence and with Roger Williams in 1636 they had a conversation with the Narragansett sachems and the Narragansett sachems agreed to give Roger Williams' party a very large piece of land that extended from Neutaconkanut Hill to the west, to Mashapaug Pond to the northwest, to above where the Pawtuxet section of Cranston is now and down to along Narragansett Bay and included that part which is now the east side of Providence, on the other side of the Providence River. That was the territory of the original town of Providence, the territory that was given to English by the sachems, by Miantunnomi, Cannonicus, and various others. And the earliest deeds that are involved in the transfer of that territory have the signatures of the sachems on them. You can see a copy of the deed for example, first Narragansett-Indian-signed deed document giving title to this land, or the usage of this land to Roger Williams signed with the mark of Cannonicus and the mark of Miantunnomi. And the English of course wrote it down in their own wording. They were very particular about these things. They had to keep written records among themselves. This is how they did it. (For facsimile of original deed see page 35.)

It says:

> *The Narragansett on the 24th of the first month, commonly called March, second year of our plantation or planting in Providence memorandum that we, Cannonicus and Miantunnomi, the two chief sachems of the Narragansett having 2 years since sold onto Roger Williams the lands and meadows upon the two fresh rivers called Mooshasuck and Woonasquatucket do now by these present do now establish and confirm the bounds of those lands from the river and fields at Pawtucket the Great Hill of Neutaconkanut on the northwest and the town of Mashapaug on the west.*

So the town of Mashapaug refers to the very large Indian community on Mashapaug that lived on that site in the early historic period.

Then came King Philip's War and one of the consequences of that war, that was a very large number of the Narragansett, particularly those living in southern Rhode Island were either killed or driven out of the area. Those who were captured at the end of the war, many of those were sent overseas to slavery or Bermuda and various other places. And many of them continued to live here. Part of the reason for that was the sachem Ninigret had been neutral during that war and therefore his lands and people weren't destroyed and the Narragansett and Niantic were very closely intermarried and

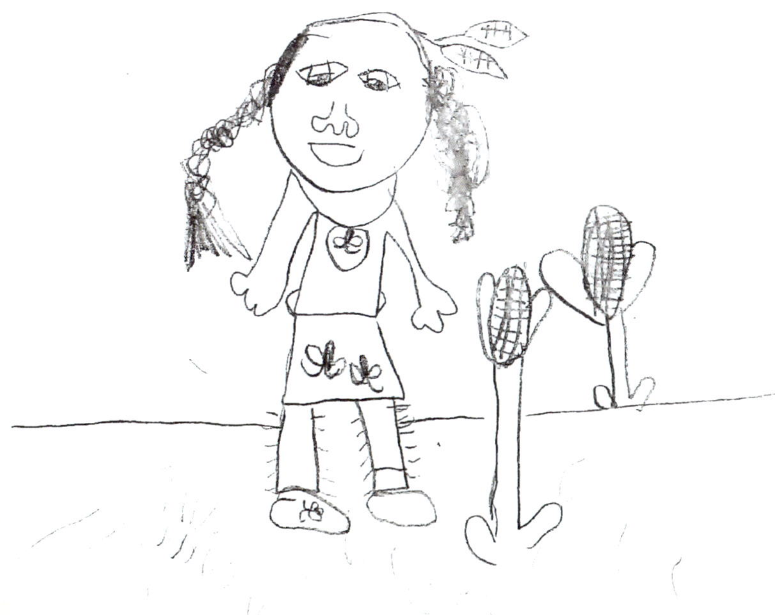

interconnected and a lot of people of Narragansett background connected with the Ninigret side of the boundary managed to survive the war, but they weren't the only ones who survived it. One of the interesting things about Indian history in Rhode Island is that there were pockets of Narragansett people that survived all over Rhode Island for one reason or another that is not even very well-known—survived the war and were not exterminated or taken into captivity. One of those communities it turns out was that community at Mashapaug. My evidence for that is this:

There was an early English settler in the town of Providence called John Howland and he lived to be a very old man and he wrote his memoirs, the different things that he remembered. In his life and recollections he says the following:

> *"The reference to the Indian tribes, the wrong impression seems to be received by many not fully conversant with the early history of New England that being that most if not all the Native Indians were exterminated or driven off to the western tribes in the war of 1675/76 whereas a great number of them never joined the hostile tribes and many others who remained neutral and joined the whites and fought on the side against their countrymen. The Sakonnet Tribe were generally allies of Colonel Church in opposition to Philip. So there were Sakonnets living in Little Compton, Rhode Island right up until this century and there are probably still other people of Sakonnet descent who may not live there any longer. Many of them continued to live in their own wigwams and others were hired and lived with the families of their white neighbors. There was a populous village of them near Mashapaug Pond. This village had the first grant of land by Miantunnomi to Roger Williams formed to the western boundary, Providence Territory. The venerable Arthur Fenner, the grandfather of Governor James Fenner, governor of Rhode Island was born in Cranston in the year 1699, 23 years after the close of Philip's War. He has informed me that when (as) a young man traveling the road from his father's house to town (which is probably Plainfield Street to Westminster Street, that's my guess reconstructing his route) it was usual to meet or pass more Indians than white people along the way."*

So that is interesting. Thus in the 1700s he's saying that in that area of Cranston between Mashapaug Pond and Cranston Street there were more Indians than whites living there at that time.

So, as far as I can tell history has been very quiet about who those people were, the generations that came and went. It is a very interesting question in fact as to how long that village community of Narragansett continued to persist. That is to say that historical records on this are pretty meager. We don't know a great deal about it.

Interestingly enough I recall, having lived in that area as a child that between the brewery, if you know that geography, between the Narragansett Brewery and Mashapaug Pond there was a very, very large neighborhood that was between Niantic Ave. and the pond. That neighborhood was made of largely one- or two-bedroom houses all mostly built by the owners, they weren't particularly elaborate houses. The streets were all paved and they were all one story or one and a half story houses with like a bedroom in the attic kind of a thing. But it was a very large community. Not knowing anything about the history of it or anything else but nevertheless to a child who simply grew up in that area and was familiar and curious about things and so forth a large number of people who lived over there were of dark colored skin, what was called in those days called colored people. And so since that's what was there, I just took it as part of the way the world was, it was just part of Providence, which it was.

But then that whole community disappeared with Route 10, all the urban renewal and the rest of that kind of stuff and is now an industrial zone. You see TV stations and warehouses and God knows what. It's kind of a wasteland of different types of industry. And you'd never know that anyone ever lived there or that there was this sort of village.

That Narragansett lived there in the 20th century became clear to me in an interview with Harold and Laura Mars in the early 1980s. They had lived there for a time in the early 1940s and had this to say about it.

***

Harold: *When we lived at Mashapug Pond there was another Indian family, down about a block, by the name of Elderkins. The Elderkins were direct descendants of the Seekonk Indians. The Seekonk Indians, of course, they lived in what is now the Wampanoag Trail. It was at East Providence. There was the Weeden family who were Narragansett and a number of them are still surviving. Most of the Indian people, to my knowledge, that attended church, I've always heard them mention and use the name Pond Street Baptist Church.*

Laura: *The Born family; they were there too. And we was all in there together and then we were living there at that time in that same community. We moved from here during the time of the war when he (Harold) was working at Quonsett Point so we went to Providence to live so to make it closer to his workplace. The Born children's mother was Hattie Cheeks from the Lantern Hill Indians and she had married this man and she lived in that section. And the Cheeks were related to my mother.*

Simmons: *So you lived over in the Mashapaug Pond area?*

Laura: *Yes we lived on what they call Tyler Street.*

Harold: *That was right off Calhoun Avenue and, in fact there's another Indian family, the Adams family.*

So the Adams family, the Born family, the Weeden family, the Marses lived in Mashapaug Pond area.

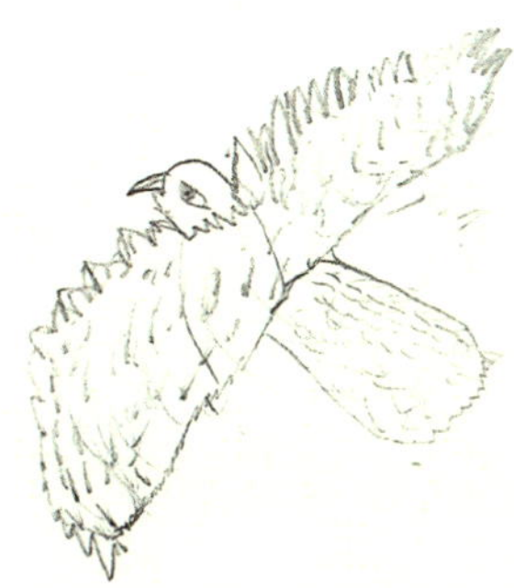

ATTRIBUTIONS

p 2 **photo** Nkéke Waupianoohom Harris

Nkéke, which means "otter" in his traditional Narragansett language, is a naturally creative, playful, and energetic little boy. At eight years old he enjoys drawing, imaginative play, watching music videos, playing outside, singing, and dancing. Nkéke has participated in Narragansett language classes and was one of the founding members of the Nahahiganseck Singers and has performed at various public events. Nkéke continues the traditions of his people as a traditional Eastern War dancer and through being a good big brother to his 2 younger siblings.

text Dawn Dove is a Nahahiganseck Elder, daughter of the family matriarch Eleanor F. Dove and the late Traditional War Chief of the Narragansett Ferris B. Dove, mother of two daughters and grandmother to eight grandchildren. Her life's work is dedicated to the continuation of the culture, language and traditions of the Nahahiganseck people. Through education, oral tradition, history, dance, song and development of cultural programs she endeavors to enlighten our world community.

p 3 **text** Dawn Dove

p 4 **collage** Nkéke Waupianoohom Harris and Robin Spears

Robin Spears, Narragansett/Niantic age 17, loves the environment and can identify invasive species and medicinal herbs. He is an artist. He is currently doing sculpture working as an apprentice to a professional sculptor. He also does a variety of traditional arts such as basketry, pottery, cornhusk doll making, beadwork and participated in painting a mural. He is a championship traditional Eastern War dancer.

text Eleanor Spears Dove, age 93 is a Niantic-Narragansett. She modeled for a painting that was exhibited at the Rhode Island School of Design in 1932 when she was in Junior High School. She and her late husband, Ferris Babcock Dove, Niantic-Narragansett, owned and operated the famous Dovecrest Restaurant in Exeter, Rhode Island for over 20 years. She has supported, advised and donated collections to Tomaquag Museum since its inception.

p 5 **collage** Nkéke Waupianoohom Harris

text Lorén Spears, age 44, Narragansett/Niantic, is the Executive Director of Tomaquag Museum. She is an educator and founded Nuweetooun School at Tomaquag Museum and served as its Director for seven years. She also is a traditional artist & arts teacher. She does beadwork, basketry, finger-weaving, leatherwork, painting, and writing. She serves her community as a Narragansett Tribal Councilwoman and Narragansett Language Committee Member.

p 6 **collage** Dawn Dove

p 7 **text** Dawn Dove

Wesly Jennings, age 19, is a Narragansett/Lakota traditional eastern woodland cedar flute player and has been performing for seven years. He is currently an enrolled college student and an intern at Tomaquag Museum where he shares what he has learned about his culture from his family to the public. He enjoys nature hikes with friends.

Dawn Dove

Eleanor Dove

p 8 **text** Lynsea Montanari carries on the traditions of her Narragansett people through song and dance. At 15 years of age she was one of the founding members of the Nahahiganseck Singing group and is a champion Eastern Blanket dancer. Lynsea excels in all academic areas with natural gifts in writing and math and a passion for science. Lynsea enjoys playing the guitar, singing contemporary music, and is a beautiful artist. As a big sister to 7 younger siblings she works to be a positive role model for each of them.

p 9 **text** Sherenté Mishitashin Harris is a traditionalist at the very young age of 11. As a young Narragansett man he continues the life ways of his people through an intense spirituality and connection to all things. Sherenté has acknowledged that he holds a responsibility to preserve the culture, traditions, language, & lifeways of his people for the next 7 generations yet to come. As a sixth grade student he excels in most all academic areas and has participated for the past 5 years in the highly capable accelerated learners program. Sherenté uses prayer in his daily life, sings with the Nahahiganseck Singing group, performs with a theatre group, and is a champion Eastern War dancer.

p 10 **photo** Sherenté Mishitashin Harris

text Lorén Spears

Ridge Spears

Ridge Spears is a Narragansett/Niantic, age 14, likes dirt-biking, video games and art. He has participated in a variety of traditional arts such as basketry, pottery, cornhusk doll making, beadwork and participated in painting a mural. He is a wonderful traditional flute player and has performed all over Southern New England.

p 11 **collage** Paulla Dove Jennings, age 71, is a Niantic-Narragansett traditional storyteller and oral historian. She has presented at universities, colleges, museums, cultural events from Alaska to Maine. She is the author of Strawberry Thanksgiving, a former tribal councilwoman, Executive Director of the RI Commission for Indian Affairs, and museum curator at both the Boston Children's Museum and Tomaquag Museum.

text Dawn Dove and Lorén Spears

p 12 **collage** Lorén Spears
text Lorén Spears
Lynsea Montanari

p 13 **collage** Lorén Spears
text Lorén Spears and Dawn Dove

p 14 **photo/collage** Lorén Spears and Lynsea Montanari
text group

p15 **photo** Lorén Spears
text group
group

p 16 **photo** Lorén Spears
text Lynsea Montanari

p 17 **photo** Lorén Spears
text Lynsea Montanari

p 18 **collage** Dawn Dove

p 19 **text** Dawn Dove

p 20 **photo** Holly Ewald, age 57, is an visual artist and educator who has developed an approach to making art that increasingly merges her studio practice with facilitating community engagement. Her interest in Indigenous communities began when she lived on a MicMac reserve in New Brunswick, Canada for two summers in the early 1970s. Since moving to Rhode Island in 1998 the history of a place has been a vital source of content for her work. She is founder of Urban Pond Procession and co-founder of Voices and Visions of Village Life. Awards include arts and humanities grants as well as an education award from the Rhode Island Historical Preservation and Heritage Commission and a Clearwater Award from The Waterfront Center in Washington, DC.

p 21 **text** Dawn Dove
Dawn Dove
Eleanor Dove
Nkéke Waupianoohom Harris

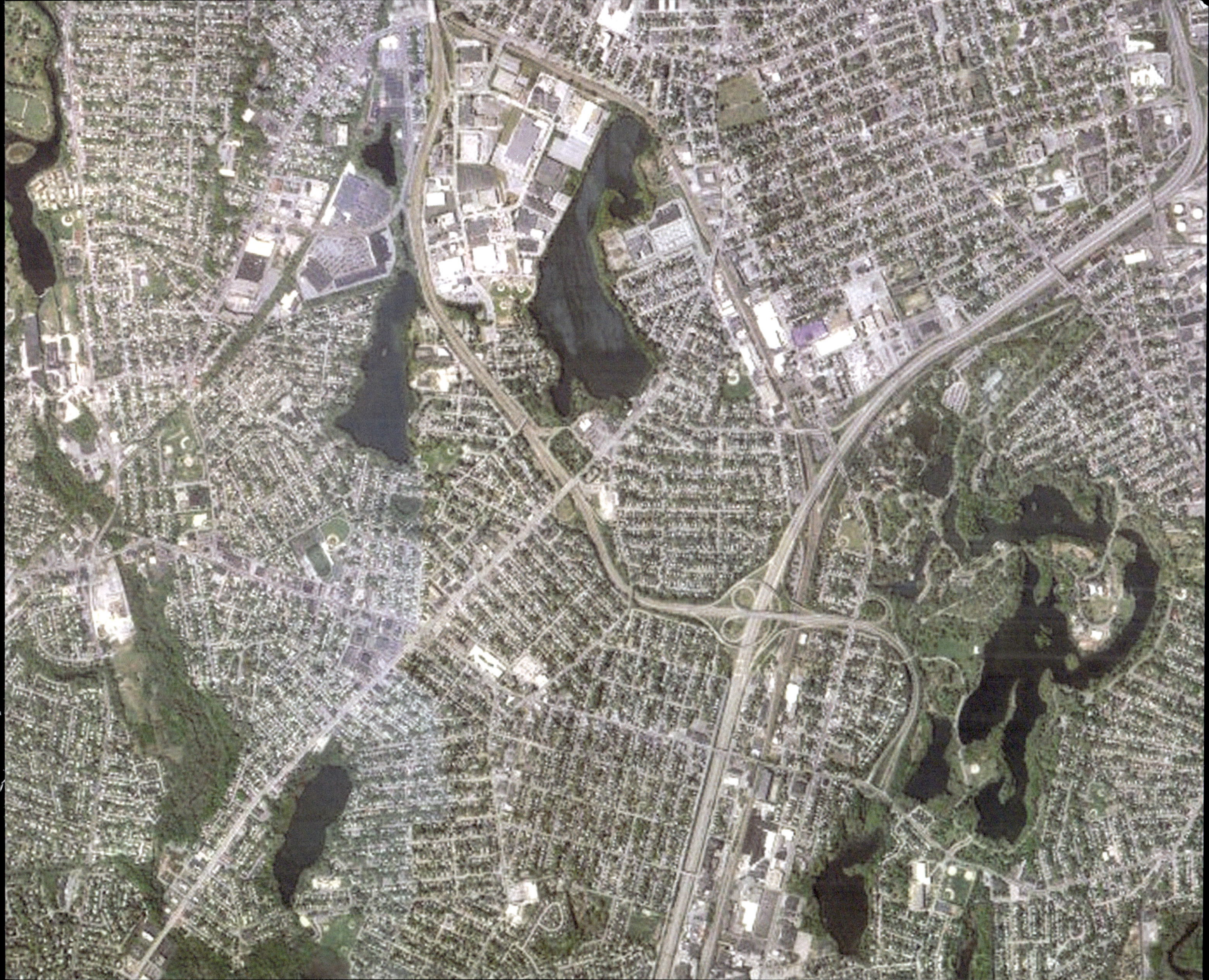

www.ingramcontent.com/pod-product-compliance
Ingram Content Group UK Ltd.
Pitfield, Milton Keynes, MK11 3LW, UK
UKRC032326290726
14090UKWH00010B/496

9781968548100

9 781968 548100